The Elementary Teacher's Guide to Parent and Student Communication

Grades 1-5

by
Jackie Carpas
Melissa Hughes
Caroline Lenzo
Kristin Oakes

Editors
Kelly Gunzenhauser
Tracy Soles

Cover Design
Todd Tyson

Table of Contents

Table of Contents

Introduction

About this Book...

Teachers and parents share the responsibility of sparking the desire to learn in children. Everyone benefits when parents and teachers build open communication to ensure the progress of their students. A crucial component of all educators' success is an ability to communicate important and sometimes difficult information to both students and parents in an effective and professional manner. The ideas, sample comments, suggestions, and reproducibles in this book will assist teachers in effectively sharing academic progress, students' strengths and weaknesses, and strategies for improvement. In short, *The Elementary Teacher's Guide to Parent and Student Communication* will help you find just the right thing to say in any situation, and will provide an easy format in which to say it.

Section Overview...

The book is divided into two main sections. The first section, **Parent and Teacher Communication Strategies**, focuses on reproducible documentation and communication forms that will enhance teacher-parent communication. This section provides a wide variety of reproducibles, including communication logs, assignment folder ideas and assignment sheets, student contracts, notes home, and conference schedule forms and suggestions. These blank templates can be easily filled in for any communication needs you may have.

When writing comments to students and parents, keeping the comments fresh and personal can be challenging. Also, writing comments about a problem a student is having is never easy. The second section of this book, **Comments for Parents and Students**, addresses many of the situations, from academic performance to social skills, that you may encounter during the school year. Several sample comments are included for each scenario, providing a variety of ways to make your meaning clear. These comments can be modified and used for report cards, interim reports, or notes home. The Comments-at-a-Glance page (page 96) offers a selection of words and phrases to insert into your own comments when you need "just the right thing to say."

Management and Documentation

All teachers, whether in their first year of teaching or their twentieth, need a good system for record keeping. Since communication is such an important element, not only of our students' success, but also in building cooperative relationships between teachers and parents, it makes sense to record every communication.

Technological advancements have increased the speed and ease of communication between home and school. E-mail (electronic mail) is an effective way to communicate with parents who have scheduling restrictions that prevent them from attending conferences or parent meetings. Many parents have e-mail accounts, and appreciate the ease and flexibility of corresponding from home or work. Many teachers also prefer communicating via e-mail because they can easily document and store records without making copies of every note sent home.

Additionally, some teachers like to use home pages (single web pages that individuals may design to display information) to post upcoming events, assignments, or schedule changes. There are very simple software programs you can use to create your own web pages with e-mail links or information for parents to easily access. While electronic communication may not be as effective as a face-to-face meeting, it provides options to those parents who may not otherwise be available.

Document each card, letter, fax, e-mail, and phone call to be sure that your students and their parents are receiving positive, helpful, and informative communication from you. Checklists can be a quick and efficient way to do this since they make documentation less time-consuming. Two reproducible checklists, The Classroom Communication Checklist and the Parent Correspondence Log, are provided in this chapter. They are the tools you need to record each contact as it occurs. Modify the checklists to meet your classroom needs.

☑ The **Classroom Communication Checklist** (page 6) is easy to use to document daily tasks and communications such as fee collections, conferences, permission slips, etc. Using one sheet, you will be able to keep track of detailed information for an entire class. Indicate the dates of phone calls or faxes to parents under the *Phone/Fax* column; dates of any notes, cards, or e-mail sent to parents under the *Mail/E-mail* column. List meeting or conference dates along with a brief comment under the *Conference* column. The *Other* column can be used to record fee collections, receipt of field trip permission slips, etc.

☑ The **Parent Correspondence Log** (page 7) is useful if you wish to make short comments to help you recall highlights of any letters, meetings, or conversations with parents. Copy a checklist for each student. Ask parents to fill in the information at the top of the form and return it to you.

Classroom Communication Checklist

Student Name	Phone/ Fax	Mail/ E-mail	Conference	Other

Parent Correspondence Log

Student's Full Name _____

Nickname (if any) _____ **Date of Birth** _____

Father's Name _____	Mother's Name _____
_____	_____
Address _____	Address _____
_____	_____
Phone (Daytime) _____	Phone (Daytime) _____
Phone (Evening) _____	Phone (Evening) _____
E-mail _____	E-mail _____
Fax _____	Fax _____
Please circle the best way above to contact you regarding non-emergency information.	**Please circle the best way above to contact you regarding non-emergency information.**

Date	Form of Communication	Comments	Follow-up

Assignment Folder

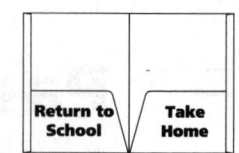

Assignment Folders can be an easy and effective intervention for students who need help learning better organizational skills and becoming more responsible for their work. Many students benefit from the structure that the Assignment Folder provides. It can be used to remind them to take materials home, to complete projects, and to study for tests. Additionally, most parents are willing and anxious to work with their children and provide the home support that they need, but are unsure of their child's assignments. The Assignment Folder can go a long way to bridge the communication gap between home and school.

To make Assignment Folders, you will need a two-pocket folder for each student. Mark one pocket on the folder *Return to School* and the other pocket *Take Home*. Then, laminate the folder for durability, and use a craft knife to cut a slit around the edge of the folder's pockets to reopen them. To keep the folder current, place a daily or weekly assignment sheet in the Return to School Pocket. Refer to the checklist below for instructions to help your students use the Assignment Folder.

The success of the Assignment Folder will depend on how well parents and students understand the importance of it and of their roles in using it. Ideally, an explanation of how to use the Assignment Folder would take place during a conference, but it could also be done at Open House, over the phone, or via a letter (a reproducible is provided on page 10) or e-mail. The time and effort you put into making sure parents and students understand how to use the folder will pay off as students become more organized and responsible for their work, and parents become partners in their children's education by being aware of the work their children are expected to do.

☑ The **Assignment Folder Take-Home Letter** reproducible (page 10) explains (or, if you have had a meeting with parents, recaps) what the Assignment Folder is and how it should be used.

☑ The **Return to School** pocket in the Assignment Folder should contain all worksheets, permission slips, and other papers students should take home to be completed and/or signed, then returned to school. Papers should be kept in this pocket until you collect them. You may wish to create a sheet of labels preprinted with *Parent/Guardian Signature:* _____, copy the sheet onto brightly colored, self-stick label paper, and attach a label to each paper in this pocket, or have children attach the labels themselves. This will make the space for the signature easy for you and parents to locate.

Assignment Folder

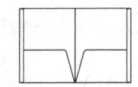

☑ The **Take Home** pocket should contain all graded assignments and practice work that is to remain at home. All work in this pocket should be removed each night and shared with parents.

☑ The **Assignment Sheet** (pages 11-12) should be used throughout the day to record all assigned work, including homework, projects, and tests. Because Assignment Sheet information is shared overnight or during the weekend, students and parents have ample opportunity to plan study time. Parents are encouraged to read and sign the Assignment Sheet at the beginning of the week to let you know they have seen it.

This reproducible can be updated daily, or once each week at the beginning or end of the week. The day(s) of the week you choose to send home the Assignment Sheet will depend on the age of your students and how you want the Assignment Sheet to function. For some children, you may wish to fill out the Assignment Sheet yourself, then copy it for each child. Or, you may prefer to model a sample Assignment Sheet for your students, and offer additional help to those students who have difficulty filling out the sheet when adding assignments. Some students may also benefit from receiving copies of the Assignment Sheet at the beginning or end of the week, then having their parents initial it each night. Older students may prefer receiving a blank Assignment Sheet to fill in on their own during school each day, then sharing it once a week with their parents. You can modify the routine of the Assignment Sheet as you see fit, and during the school year, you may choose to change how often the Assignment Sheet must be reviewed and signed by parents.

Dear Parents,

The students in our class will be using an Assignment Folder to keep track of all of the papers they need to keep at home, and all of the ones they need to return to school. Below is an explanation of how to help your child use the Assignment Folder to keep track of homework, tests, projects, and other papers. Please sign the Assignment Sheet each week so that you can help your child plan for study time, and check both pockets of the folder each night for important papers. I will check folders each week for parents' signatures! Your interest, support, and encouragement are essential to the success of the Assignment Folder. Thank you for your cooperation!

Sincerely,

_____
Teacher Signature

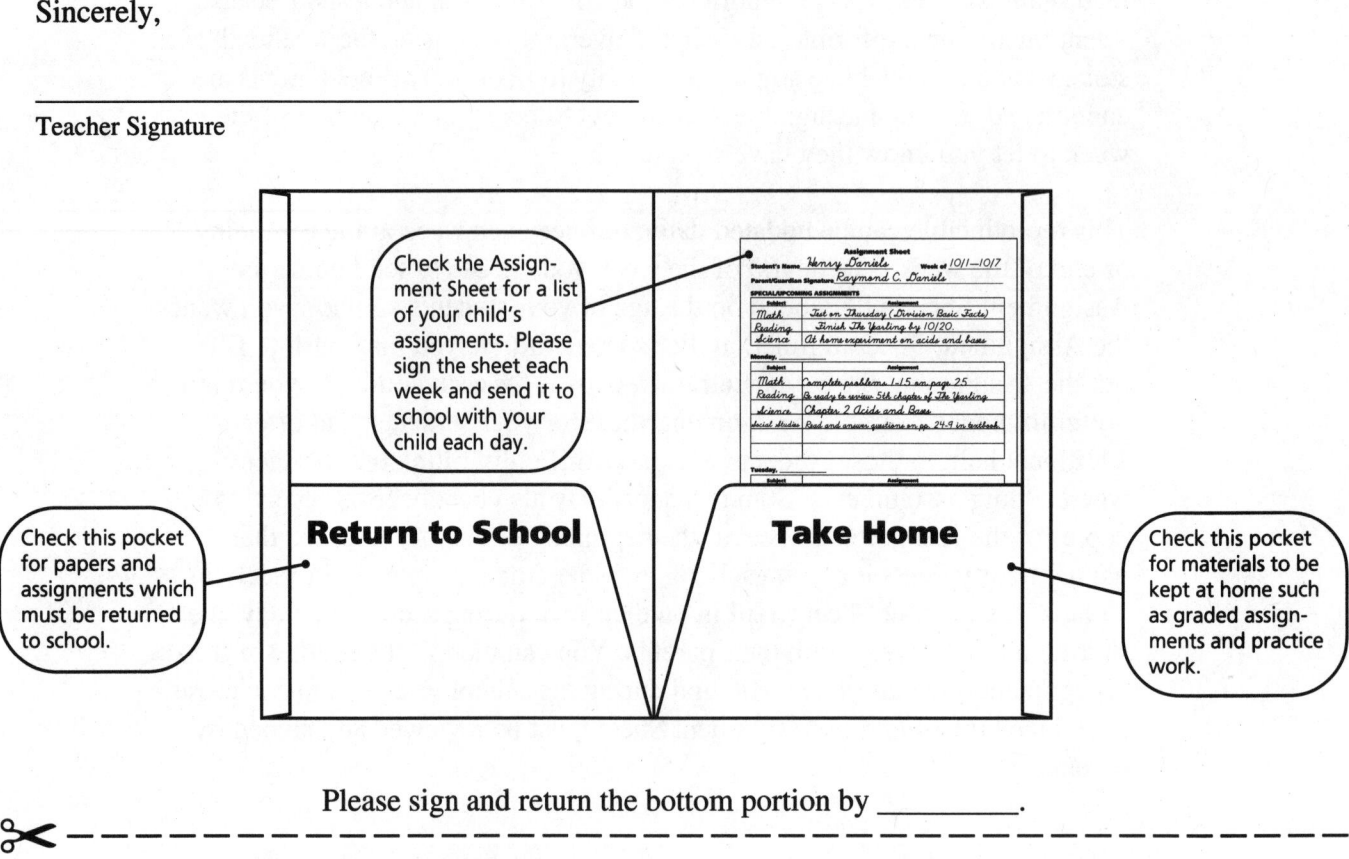

Please sign and return the bottom portion by _____.

- -

Assignment Folder Response

I have seen the Assignment Sheet and Assignment Folder, and I understand how to help my child use the folder to keep papers organized. I also understand that it is my child's responsibility to explain the contents of the folder, and to remember to get my signature on each Assignment Sheet and on any other pages which require it.

_____   _____
Parent Signature   Date

Assignment Sheet

Student's Name_____   **Week of** _____

Parent/Guardian Signature_____

SPECIAL/UPCOMING ASSIGNMENTS

Subject	Assignment

Monday, _____

Subject	Assignment

Tuesday, _____

Subject	Assignment

Wednesday, _____

Subject	Assignment

Thursday, _____

Subject	Assignment

Friday, _____

Subject	Assignment

Contracts

It is often difficult, though necessary, to find time each day to call or write letters to parents regarding their children's behavior or progress. Reproducible contracts provide a streamlined yet formal way to address any concern.

Contracts also help to clarify the goals that the child, parent, and teacher are working to improve. Contracts set up as frequency charts offer a consistent way to report and measure daily and weekly performance. They can help illustrate to children and parents how often undesirable behavior (hitting, poor grades, not paying attention, etc.) occurs, and can serve as a concrete record of improvement. A frequency format often helps children monitor their behavior throughout the day and can motivate them to improve.

Keeping contracts as simple as possible, and relying on check marks or tally marks will help make this process more manageable for everyone. When designing a contract for a student, keep the following points in mind:

- Limit the number of behaviors to be addressed.
- Be clear about rules, goals, and expectations.
- Change goals and expectations as needed by issuing a new contract.
- Brainstorm a list of rewards and consequences with the child. Rewards will be more valuable and consequences will be more fair if the child has input.
- Agree on rewards and consequences before the contract begins.
- If possible, have rewards and consequences take place at school and at home.
- Keep in mind that short-term goals are desirable for immediate feedback; however, long-term goals can help sustain interest and serve as motivation to form new habits.
- Give the child more than one chance to fail before consequences begin, especially in the beginning. Remember, success breeds success.
- Assign responsibilities for goal-reaching to each of the people involved (child, parent, and teacher), so that all three are part of the improvement process.
- If something is not working, change it! This is your plan, so do what works.

☑ The **Spelling Contract** (page 15) is a short-term contract geared to a child's improvement in spelling, as the example shows. With modifications, it can be used for other subjects, including math, social studies, and vocabulary words. There are blank spaces for words, bonus words, and a checklist of ways to help a child practice spelling. A space for a parent signature is included at the bottom, as well as a place to indicate how the student has studied. Space is also provided to list rewards and consequences, although if learning rather than improving a grade or test score is the focus, you may not wish to list consequences.

Contracts

☑ The **Math Facts Contract** (page 16), also a weekly contract, can be used to help drill children in learning fact families for all simple math operations. It can also be modified to help students memorize fraction and decimal conversions, skip counting, and even simple formulas. It is similar to the spelling contract in that it offers adjustable rules of study and space for rewards, consequences, and parent signatures.

☑ The **Goal-Based Contract** (page 17) is a very open-ended frequency contract which can address both academic and behavioral concerns. Any goal that teachers want students to reach can be written into the goal area at the top of the page. Spaces for dates and record-keeping of progress are provided, as is a space for rewards and consequences.

☑ The **Daily Behavior Report Contract** (page 18) can be helpful for students with general behavior problems who need frequent feedback. Teachers, parents, and students are encouraged to use this contract on a daily basis.

☑ The **Student Grade Contract** (page 19) effectively demonstrates for students and parents how effort and assignment completion affect academic performance. Students are given a check for assignments that are completed on time, as well as a check for assignments which show good effort (are neat, have problems done correctly, etc.). You can choose how many checks a student needs to receive a reward.

A sample of each contract with the information filled in is shown (pages 20-21).

Name: _____   Date: _____

SPELLING CONTRACT

Goals of this contract:

_____'s goal is to _____

_____.

Contract Terms:

✔ The student promises to practice his/her spelling words each night at home with a family member, using at least one of the following methods.

1   Spelling the words aloud when they are pronounced to him/her.
2   Writing the words when they are pronounced to him/her.
3   Using each of the words in a sentence.
4   Writing each of the words at least two times.

Spelling Words for this week:

_____   _____   _____   _____

_____   _____   _____   _____

_____   _____   _____   _____

_____   _____   _____   _____

Bonus or Extra Credit Words for this week:

_____   _____   _____

Incentives:

If the student meets the goal stated above, then he/she can _____

_____.

Consequences:

If the student does not meet the goal stated above, then he/she will _____

_____.

Contract Accepted by:

Student _____

Teacher _____

Parents* _____

*Each night this week, please circle which methods from the contract terms listed above your child used to study spelling words, then sign your initials and date in the box beside the correct day.	Mon.	1	2	3	4	
	Tue.	1	2	3	4	
	Wed.	1	2	3	4	
	Thur.	1	2	3	4	
	Fri.	1	2	3	4	

Name: _____ Date: _____

MATH FACTS CONTRACT

Goals of this contract:

◎ _____'s goal is to _____

_____ .

Contract Terms:

✓ The student promises to practice his/her math facts three times per week at home with a family member, using at least one of the following methods.

1 Using flash cards   4 Playing a math computer game
2 Writing number families   5 Using manipulatives
3 Taking a timed practice test   6 Other _____

Math Facts for this week:

_____   _____   _____   _____

_____   _____   _____   _____

_____   _____   _____   _____

_____   _____   _____   _____

Bonus or Extra Credit Math Facts for this week:

_____   _____   _____   _____

Incentives:

☺ If the student meets the goal stated above, then he/she can _____

_____ .

Consequences:

☹ If the student does not meet the goal stated above, then he/she will _____

_____ .

Contract Accepted by:

Student _____

Teacher _____

Parents* _____

*For each night this week that your child studied math facts, please circle which methods your child used, then sign your initials and date in the box beside the correct day.	Mon.	1	2	3	4	5	6	
	Tue.	1	2	3	4	5	6	
	Wed.	1	2	3	4	5	6	
	Thur.	1	2	3	4	5	6	
	Fri.	1	2	3	4	5	6	

Name: _____   Date: _____

GOAL-BASED CONTRACT

Goals of this contract:

_____'s goal is to _____
_____.

Contract Terms:

✓ Each check a student receives will count toward the total goal of _____ checks.
Actual checks received: _____.

Days on which goal was reached:

Week of:	Mon.	Tue.	Wed.	Thur.	Fri.	Comments
_____						
_____						
_____						
_____						

Incentives:

If the student meets the goal stated above, then he/she can _____
_____.

Consequences:

If the student does not meet the goal stated above, then he/she will _____
_____.

Contract Accepted by:

Student _____

Teacher _____

Parents _____

Name: _____   Date: _____

DAILY BEHAVIOR REPORT CONTRACT

Goals of this contract:

◎ _____'s goal is to _____

_____ .

Contract Terms:

✓ Each time a rule is broken, its number will be written in appropriate box. Please sign this form **each week** and return it to school with your child.

Behavior rules for this contract:

1. _____

2. _____

3. _____

4. _____

5. _____

Week of:	Mon.	Tue.	Wed.	Thur.	Fri.	Comments	Parent Initials
_____							
_____							
_____							
_____							

Incentives:

☺ If the student meets the goal stated above, then he/she can _____

_____ .

Consequences:

☹ If the student does not meet the goal stated above, then he/she will _____

_____ .

Contract Accepted by:

Student _____

Teacher _____

Parents _____

Name: _____   Date: _____

STUDENT GRADE CONTRACT

Goals of this contract:

◎ _____'s goal is to _____
_____.

On-Track Contract Terms:

✔ The student will receive a "✓" or an "x" in each area below for each listed assignment. A "✓" under the Effort column indicates that work was done neatly and correctly. A "✓" under the Completed on Time column indicates that all work was completed by the assignment due date.

Subject:	Assignment:	Effort:	Completed:
_____	_____	_____	_____
_____	_____	_____	_____
_____	_____	_____	_____
_____	_____	_____	_____
_____	_____	_____	_____
_____	_____	_____	_____
_____	_____	_____	_____

Bonus or Extra Credit Assignments for this week:

_____	_____	_____	_____
_____	_____	_____	_____
_____	_____	_____	_____

Total checks earned for this week: _____

Incentives:

☺ If the student meets the goal stated above, then he/she can _____
_____.

Consequences:

☹ If the student does not meet the goal stated above, then he/she will _____
_____.

Contract accepted by:

Student _____

Teacher _____

Parents _____

Name: *Ray Howard* **Date:** *November 10, 2008*

SPELLING CONTRACT

Goals of this contract:

Ray's goal is to *spell 8 out of 10 spelling words correctly this week (the week of 11/13/00)*

Contract Terms:

✓ The student promises to practice his/her spelling words each night at home with a family member, using at least one of the following methods.

1 Spelling the words aloud when they are pronounced to him/her.
2 Writing the words when they are pronounced to him/her.
3 Using each of the words in a sentence.
4 Writing each of the words at least two times.

Spelling Words for this week:

I'm	*won't*	*wasn't*	*he's*
wouldn't	*I'd*	*aren't*	*shouldn't*
couldn't	*she's*		

Bonus or Extra Credit Words for this week:

let's	*o'clock*

Incentives:

If the student meets the goal stated above, then he/she can *have two gold stars for the spelling chart*

Consequences:

If the student does not meet the goal stated above, then he/she will *study the spelling words he misses and be tested on them during next week's spelling test*

Contract Accepted by:

Student *Ray Howard*

Teacher *Mr. Erik Wheeler*

Parents* *Mrs. Jill Howard*

*Each night this week, please circle which methods from the contract terms listed above your child used to study spelling words, then sign your initials and the date in the box beside the correct day.

	1	2	3	4	
Mon.	①	2	3	4	JH 11/13
Tue.	1	②	③	4	JH 11/14
Wed.	①	2	3	④	JH 11/15
Thur.	①	②	3	4	JH 11/16
Fri.	1	2	3	4	test day!

Name: *Tara Delaney* **Date:** *September 18, 2006*

GOAL-BASED CONTRACT

Goals of this contract:

Tara's goal is to *turn in all of her classwork and homework*

Contract Terms:

✓ Each check a student receives will count toward the total goal of ___16___ checks.
Actual checks received: ___16___ .

Days on which goal was reached:

Week of:	Mon.	Tue.	Wed.	Thur.	Fri.	Comments
9/18-9/22	✓	✓		✓	✓	Good!
9/25-9/29		✓			✓	Room for improvement.
10/2-10/6	✓		✓	✓	✓	Keep working!
10/9-10/13	✓	✓	✓	✓	✓	Perfect! Hope you are hungry!

Incentives:

If the student meets the goal stated above, then he/she can *share a special lunch with the teacher*

Consequences:

If the student does not meet the goal stated above, then he/she will *attend a conference with her parents to review why assignments were missed*

Contract Accepted by:

Student *Tara Delaney*

Teacher *Ms. Betty Neville*

Parents *Mrs. Janelle Delaney Mr. Taylor Delaney*

Name: *Lynette Gamble* **Date:** *September 8, 2005*

MATH FACTS CONTRACT

Goals of this contract:

Lynette's goal is to *memorize all facts in the twos multiplication table*

Contract Terms:

✓ The student promises to practice his/her math facts three times per week at home with a family member, using at least one of the following methods.

1 Using flash cards
2 Writing number families
3 Taking a timed practice test
4 Playing a math computer game
5 Using manipulatives
6 Other _____

Math Facts for this week:

2 x 0 = 0	2 x 1 = 2	2 x 2 = 4	2 x 3 = 6
2 x 4 = 8	2 x 5 = 10	2 x 6 = 12	2 x 7 = 14
2 x 8 = 16	2 x 9 = 18		

Bonus or Extra Credit Math Facts for this week:

2 x 10 = 20	2 x 11 = 22	2 x 12 = 24

Incentives:

If the student meets the goal stated above, then he/she can *choose the recess game for the day*

Consequences:

If the student does not meet the goal stated above, then he/she will *write out the multiplication facts family for 2s three times*

Contract Accepted by:

Student *Lynette Gamble*

Teacher *Mrs. Allison Bassony*

Parents *Mrs. Amanda Gamble*

*For each night this week that your child studied math facts, please circle which methods your child used, then sign your initials and the date in the box beside the correct day.

	1	2	3	4	5	6	
Mon.	①	2	3	④	5	6	AB 9/11
Tue.	1	②	3	4	⑤	6	AB 9/12
Wed.	①	2	③	4	5	6	AB 9/13
Thur.	1	2	③	4	5	6	AB 9/14
Fri.	1	2	3	4	5	6	test day!

Name: *Maria Smith*   Date: *August 18, 2007*

DAILY BEHAVIOR REPORT CONTRACT

Goals of this contract:

◎ *Maria* 's goal is to *break fewer than three rules per week* .

Contract Terms:

✓ Each time a rule is broken, its number will be written in appropriate box. Please sign this form **each week** and return it to school with your child.

Behavior rules for this contract:

1. *Do not talk during reading time.*
2. *Keep your hands to yourself.*
3. *Raise your hand before you contribute to class discussions.*
4. *Pay attention during filmstrips.*
5. *Do not break into the lunch line.*

Week of:	Mon.	Tue.	Wed.	Thur.	Fri.	Comments	Parent Initials
8/21-8/25	1,4	3,5	2	2	3	*This was a hard week! Next week will be better.*	C.S.
8/28-9/1	1	3,5	2	2		*Keep trying!*	C.S.
9/4-9/8	Labor Day	2	1			*You're doing better!*	C.S.
9/11-9/15	1	3				*Great improvement!*	C.S.

Incentives:

☺ If the student meets the goal stated above, then he/she can *choose a special prize from the prize box* .

Consequences:

☹ If the student does not meet the goal stated above, then he/she will *attend a conference with her parents about how to improve her behavior.* .

Contract Accepted by:

Student *Maria Smith*

Teacher *Mr. Martin Duggins*

Parents *Mrs. Cecillia Smith*

Name: *Edward Roberts*   Date: *January 12, 2001*

STUDENT GRADE CONTRACT

Goals of this contract:

◎ *Edward's* 's goal is to *earn 8 checks this week* .

On-Track Contract Terms:

✓ The student will receive a "✓" or an "x" in each area below for each listed assignment. A "✓" under the Effort column indicates that work was done neatly and correctly. A "✓" under the Completed on Time column indicates that all of the work was completed by the assignment due date.

Subject:	Assignment:	Effort:	Completed on Time:
Math	*Page 25, Problems 1-12*	✓	x
Spelling	*Unit 6, Part 2*	✓	✓
Social Studies	*Worksheet*	x	✓
Science	*Questions in Chapter 2*	✓	✓
Reading	*Questions in Chapter 3*	✓	✓

Bonus or Extra Credit Assignments for this week:

Spelling	*Extra credit words from Unit 6, Part 1*	✓	✓

Total checks earned for this week: *10*

Incentives:

☺ If the student meets the goal stated above, then he/she can *have 20 extra minutes of art time and 15 extra minutes of free reading time* .

Consequences:

☹ If the student does not meet the goal stated above, then he/she will *lose 15 minutes of recess each week until a new student grade contract is fulfilled* .

Contract accepted by:

Student *Edward Roberts*

Teacher *Mr. Brandon Russell*

Parents *Mrs. Linda Roberts*

Notes Home

Effective communication is essential for students' academic and social growth. A simple note home relating news about a good test score, acknowledging a birthday celebration, or expressing concern about a student conveys caring and responsibility. This attitude is fundamental to building strong relationships with students and parents. While parents need to know of problems that arise, they also appreciate short notes acknowledging daily successes.

Keeping parents up-to-date does not have to be a time-consuming task. Use the Notes Home reproducibles and the following tips to make sending notes home a more effective and convenient way of communicating.

- ☑ **Get-to-Know-You Letter** (page 25) answers a lot of those "beginning-of-the-year" questions you may have about your students. This form shows parents that you are taking the time to learn about their children at the beginning of the year. It will also help you plan for any special circumstances, and learn about your class as a whole. You may wish to mail these forms before the school year begins and then collect them at Open House or Meet the Teachers night, or pass them out at one of these events and have parents return them to you by a certain date.

- ☑ **Student Postcards** (page 26) sent to a student's home are effective because young students may seldom get mail that is addressed to them. Postcards are an inexpensive way to brighten a student's day, while at the same time making sure that parents get your message as well. This section includes a page of postcards designed to be enlarged to approximately 135% (standard postcard size is 4" x 6"), copied onto card stock, cut apart, and mailed to students. To cut down on time spent addressing the postcards, print students' names and addresses on a few sets of labels. As you use the labels, you will also have a record of which students have not received postcards.

- ☑ **Notes to Parents** (pages 27-28) can be sent home with students or mailed directly to parents. Depending on the nature of the note, you may want to retain a copy for your files. To retain a copy of a note sent to a parent, use carbon paper or a pressure-sensitive form to duplicate a message as you write it, or use a copy machine and send the parent the original.

☑ **Quick Notes** (no reproducible) help you communicate to parents during the rush of the school day. Preprint comments on half-sheets of paper so that you simply have to fill in the blanks. Label file folders *Good News, Shows Improvement*, etc. In the folders, place notes that read: ____ *had a great day!* or *What an improvement!* ____ *has been working hard in* ____ *and it shows!* or ____ *is missing the following assignments:* ___. Store stickers in the folders, and use them to decorate the forms. Refer to the Comments section of this book (pages 36-95) and adjust comments to fit your needs.

☑ **Friendly Letters** (no reproducible) involves students doing their share of communicating with their parents. Each Friday afternoon, have children write letters to their parents informing them about school and class events of the past week. Model a letter for the class, and ask for students' input. Suggest that they tell parents about in-class videos, field trips, new units of study, new students, and upcoming test dates. You can even use the letter writing process as a tool for teaching students how to write friendly letters, how to print or write in cursive, and how to recognize and use good sentence structure.

☑ **Listening Logs** (no reproducible), notebooks which act as student journals, allow students to reflect on lessons learned and their thoughts on the school day. You can allot ten minutes each day for students to reflect on a lesson, an activity, or their feelings about the day. After writing time is up, collect the logs and respond to each student, reinforcing good efforts made and using encouraging comments to help the child do better. Once a week, send the logs home and ask parents to read the entries, write comments of their own, and sign the logs, then send them back to school with their children.

☑ A **Travelling Totebag** (no reproducible) invites students and parents to communicate with you from home. Inside the totebag, include a pencil, a folder of looseleaf paper, and a note of explanation. The note should tell students and parents what topic to write about in their entries, such as a chapter being read in class, thoughts on lunchroom rules, new math concepts, etc. Encourage students and parents to write down questions and comments on the paper. Then, students should return the totebag and its contents for your response. Write your responses on the pages with the students' writing, so they can review their comments while reading yours. After students and parents read your reply, they should return the totebag to you, complete with the original contents. Remove the looseleaf paper, file it in a three-ring binder which you keep, and repeat the process with the next child. Each time you send the travelling totebag home with a child, you may want to also send that child's previous entries for the parents review. Once all parents and children have responded to the chosen topic, start over with a new one!

☑ **Classroom Calendars** (no reproducible) will help keep parents and students on top of upcoming school activities. At the beginning of each month, fill in a calendar with test dates, project due dates, field trips, birthdays, and any other special events. Send home a copy with each student, so that parents and students will have important dates at their fingertips.

☑ Allowing children to help produce a **Weekly Classroom Bulletin** or **Newsletter** (no reproducible) is another great way to involve children in keeping parents informed about their classroom. Use publishing software to create a flexible bulletin format. Sections of the weekly bulletin might include student birthdays, an *Author's Corner* (where student work is showcased), *Hot Happenings in Room #_____*, *Special Events*, *Recommended Reading* (a list of class favorites), and *Volunteers Needed*. After you have established a format, familiarize older students with the bulletin so that they can easily make weekly changes themselves.

Deciding when to send home the bulletin will depend on whether you want it to be a recap of the previous week or a tool to inform parents of upcoming events. If you send the bulletin home on a Friday, students will have an opportunity during the week to practice summarizing the week's events before putting them into a newsletter. On the other hand, a Monday bulletin will inform parents of upcoming events and help prepare students for the week ahead.

Dear Parents,

I would like to know more about your child so that I can better meet his or her individual needs. Please take a moment to complete this **Get-to-know-you** letter and return it to me by _____.

Child's Name _____
Parents' Names _____
_____
Phone Number _____
Best time to be reached _____

Thank you, _____
                    Teacher Signature

1. What motivates your child? _____

   _____

2. What kinds of things upset your child? _____

   _____

3. List five words that best describe your child's character and/or personality: _____

   _____

4. My child's areas of strength are: _____

5. My child struggles with: _____

6. How would you rate your child's attitude toward school? 1   2   3   4   5
                                          Needs Improvement ←————→ Super

7. How would you rate your child's sense of responsibility? 1   2   3   4   5
                                          Needs Improvement ←————→ Super

8. Are there any personal or medical problems of which I should be aware? This information will be shared with the school nurse if medication is involved. _____

   _____

9. Do you have any additional comments or concerns? _____

   _____

_____   _____
Parent Signature   Date

Thank you for completing this form. I know that together we can make this year successful for your child.

Happy Birthday to You!

_____
_____
_____
_____
_____
_____

Have a great vacation!

_____
_____
_____
_____
_____
_____

Welcome Back to School!

_____
_____
_____
_____
_____
_____

Guess what happened at school today!

_____
_____
_____
_____
_____
_____

From the Desk of:

_____

Date: _____

_____

_____

_____

_____

_____

_____

Teacher: _____ Parent: _____

Please sign and return this form. You are welcome to write comments on the back of this sheet. Thank you!

- -

From the Desk of:

_____

Date: _____

I am so proud of _____

because_____

_____

_____

_____

_____

A Note From the Teacher

Date: _____

_____

_____

_____

_____

_____

_____ I would like to schedule a conference   _____ A conference is not necessary at this time

Teacher Signature: _____

Please write your comments below and return the lower portion to the teacher. Thank you!

Parent/Guardian Response

PLEASE
SIGN AND
RETURN

Date: _____

_____

_____

_____

_____

_____

Parent/Guardian Signature: _____

Conferences

Conferences provide a wonderful opportunity for parents and teachers to get to know each other and discuss the children they share. For all conferences, especially the first one, you can make a good first impression by being organized and on time. Being prepared reduces your anxiety and maximizes your meeting time by allowing you to focus on sharing information about your students and building a partnership between home and school.

Parents may be nervous and apprehensive at conference time. They may expect to receive negative news. With planning and extra effort on your part, you can create an atmosphere that puts them at ease. Consider the following ideas:

- First, make sure that your classroom is neat and organized. Your students will be willing participants in cleanup activities such as straightening desks and cleaning chalkboards. Bulletin boards should be current and have plenty of samples of student work. Room air freshener will also add a nice touch.
- Second, arrange to have a pre-conference waiting area with a table, comfortable, adult-sized chairs, class books, and projects for parents to look through. Post a schedule and provide a clock, and encourage waiting parents to knock on your door if a conference is running over the scheduled time.
- Third, be on time, and have materials ready and organized. Provide samples of each child's work, and have your grade books available. Also, pull a set of textbooks so that you can point out important features if needed.
- Fourth, begin by sharing the student's strengths and successes. It can be hard to discuss troublesome areas, but parents will appreciate your honesty and concern. Have a strategy or two ready to share with parents to improve weak areas. With parents, brainstorm ideas to help their child improve, then agree on a plan of action and future means of communication.

Finally, although you will find that the vast majority of the parents you meet and conference with will be cooperative and supportive, at some time in your career you will probably have a conference with a difficult parent. Preparation is most important in this situation. As with any conference, plan the points you wish to cover, and have work samples and documented anecdotal records to illustrate what you are saying. Be factual, and do not focus on your feelings or opinions.

When anticipating a difficult conference, don't hesitate to ask another teacher or administrator to sit in. Sometimes having other people present helps keep the discussion focused on student rather than teacher behavior. If parents become abusive, loud, or use inappropriate language, ask them to stop. If they are unable or unwilling to comply, end the conference and invite them to reschedule. Strive to be professional and maintain your composure. Do not argue. It may be necessary to "agree to disagree," so record differing opinions on the Conference Summary (page 35) to be signed by both of you. After a difficult conference, alert an administrator or the school principal, and keep a written summary of the events.

☑ The **Parent-Teacher Conference Schedule** (page 31) can be a real timesaver for you, especially if your school has scheduled conference days or evenings. You may want to take advantage of a time when parents are gathered at school, such as Open House or Meet the Teachers night, in order to have parents sign up on the Parent-Teacher Conference Schedule for a time that is convenient for them, even though there may be some time between events. This will give parents time to coordinate other events, and you will only have the remaining, empty slots to schedule after the Open House night is over.

☑ The **Conference Request** form (page 32) should be sent to parents who have not already scheduled a conference during your school's designated conference times, or to parents whom you feel you need to see. Having parents schedule conferences beforehand (see above) will reduce the number of letters you need to send.

☑ The **Conference Confirmation** form (page 33) serves as a reminder to all parents who previously signed up for a conference. It also allows you to re-schedule conferences with any parents who are unable to come at their previously chosen time.

☑ The **Pre-Conference Questionnaire for Parents** (page 34) is a helpful tool for planning a successful conference. It provides parents with an opportunity to plan anything they wish to discuss with you, and includes space for them to write down any specific questions. Having this information ahead of time relieves anxiety because you are aware of the parents' concerns prior to the conference. You will be able to gather needed materials, such as classwork, and list the topics to be discussed on your summary form. Often, you will find that you and the parents have the same concerns! If parents neglect to return the questionnaire, follow up with a note home (page 28) or phone call (record on the Parent Correspondence Log (page 7).

☑ The **Conference Summary Form** (page 35) actually saves time prior to the conference because you can check off the concerns you have, as well as those the parents noted on the Pre-Conference Questionnaire for Parents (page 34, see above) before the conference begins. A summary of the conference and the agreed-upon strategies can be filled in during the conference. At the end of each conference, both you and the parents should sign the summary form, and each of you should have a copy to keep for your records. This way, documentation is complete by the end of the conference. It is also wise to use this form for telephone conferences because it helps you organize your thoughts, and helps to document the parent contact and agreed-upon strategies. A copy of this form can then be sent to parents as well.

 # Parent-Teacher Conference Schedule

Teacher _____

Date _____

Time	Student's Name	Parent's Name(s)	Confirmed?

Conferences

Conference Request Form

From the Desk of:

_____

Date: _____

Dear _____,

I would like to schedule a conference with you as soon as possible. Please indicate on the bottom portion of this form when we can meet. Thank you!

Sincerely,

_____
Teacher Signature

Please fill out the bottom portion of this form and return it to the teacher. Thank you!

- -

Conference Request Form Reply

Child's Name: _____

Parent's Name: _____

Telephone #: _____

Below are the times and dates that I am free to meet with you for a conference.

First Choice: _____

Second Choice: _____

Third Choice: _____

Best time to contact me: _____

_____
Parent Signature

_____
Date

Conference Confirmation

Teacher: _____ **Date:** _____

To the Parent of: _____

A conference has been scheduled for you on _____, from _____ until _____, in room # _____. I am looking forward to having an opportunity to discuss your child's progress with you. Feel free to call the school if you have questions.

Sincerely,

_____
Teacher Signature

Please cut the bottom portion of this form and return it to the teacher.

- -

Conference Confirmation Reply

_____   Yes, I am planning to attend the scheduled conference.

_____   Sorry, I will be unable to attend the scheduled conference. Please contact me to reschedule. The best date and time to contact me is _____.

Student's Name _____

Parent's Name _____

Phone Number _____

Date _____

 # Pre-Conference Questionnaire for Parents

To the parents of: _____ **Date:** _____

Dear Parents:

I am looking forward to seeing you at your scheduled conference on _____. Please take a few minutes to complete the following information about your child, then return this form to me. This will help me prepare to address any concerns and answer any questions you may have during our conference.

Sincerely, _____
<u>Teacher Signature</u>

1. Please list any concerns you have about your child's academic performance: _____

   _____

   _____

   _____

2. Please list any concerns you have about your child's social performance: _____

   _____

   _____

   _____

3. Please list any other questions or comments you have about your child that you would like to discuss in a conference: _____

   _____

   _____

   _____

Conference Summary Form

Student: _____ **Date:** _____

Personal Conference _____ **Telephone Conference** _____ **Grade** _____

Attendees: _____

The following information was shared with parents:

Behavior
_____ Consistently well-behaved
_____ Improved classroom behavior
_____ Unacceptable classroom behavior
_____ Well-mannered
_____ Fine social skills
_____ Sets good example for others

Effort
_____ Hard worker
_____ Motivated learner
_____ Displays sense of responsibility
_____ Follows directions
_____ Does not follow directions
_____ Needs to improve participation
_____ Rushes through assignments
_____ Listening skills need improvement
_____ Poor effort
_____ Poor attitude toward learning

Organization
_____ Uses time effectively
_____ Organized
_____ Disorganized
_____ Lacking the following materials:_____
_____

Academic Performance
_____ Standardized test results
_____ Report card information
_____ Improved academic performance
_____ Study skills need improvement
_____ Incomplete or missing homework
_____ Incomplete or missing makeup work
_____ Absences hindering progress
_____ Poor/failing quiz/test scores

Other
_____ _____
_____ _____

Strategies for Improvement:
_____ Implement contract
_____ Continue current contract
_____ Parent/Teacher to check assignments
_____ Provide a consistent place and time to study
_____ Must improve organization
_____ Must complete work on time
_____ Replace the following supplies: _____
_____
_____ Have the student write a plan or strategy to improve
_____ Follow up meeting on Date/Time: _____
_____ Will provide practice at home
_____ Other: _____
_____
_____
_____

Teacher Comments:

Parent Comments:

_____ _____
Teacher Signature   Parent Signature

Comments

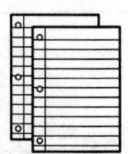

This section is devoted to comments that you can use to communicate successes or concerns on report cards, interim reports, and notes home. The comments cover almost every area that you may need to address. They are divided into categories to make it easy to find the right phrase to convey the appropriate message. Comments for both students and parents are included.

Comments are provided for those students who are doing well, who are improving, and those who need strategies to correct or improve performance. The *Well Done* comments are geared toward the parents of students who are exceptional in an area, or who have worked successfully to overcome difficulty in that area. The *Is Improving* comments reinforce continued progress, while letting parents and students know that improvement is still necessary. *Needs Improvement* comments identify a need for action on the part of the student, parent, and teacher, in order to improve poor performance or unacceptable behavior. *Comments for Students* are geared toward students only.

These comments are intended to be a starting point. They can be modified or combined for each individual situation. You may also wish to consult the Comments-at-a-Glance list (page 96) for a variety of word choices.

Behavior

Character

- ❑ Lying
- ❑ Stealing
- ❑ Cheating
- ❑ Sharing
- ❑ Attitude and Respect
- ❑ Citizenship

Lying

Is Improving
Thank you for our recent conference regarding ___. He seems to understand the importance of honesty and is trying hard to improve. Together, I feel we can help him continue to make progress in this area.

Lying (continued)

Is Improving

Our conversations about ___ have been helpful. She has made a conscious effort to tell the truth, even in difficult situations. I am proud of her progress.

I am very pleased with the social growth ___ is demonstrating. He is trying hard to tell the truth, and I think he is beginning to see the value of honesty.

Since our last conversation, ___ has made progress in understanding how lies can hurt other people. Her peer relations have improved, and I'm proud of her.

Needs Improvement

___ has been experiencing problems with his peers lately. He has been fabricating stories about others, and these untrue statements are causing hurt feelings. I am sure that you want ___ to have positive peer relations, and I know you value honesty. Let's get together to discuss this issue with ___.

I am concerned about ___. She has been dishonest with her peers and me about her work and belongings. When can we meet to discuss some strategies that we could use together that may help her?

___ still seems to have difficulty telling the truth. Please help me reinforce the importance of honesty by speaking with him, and reviewing his contract and the consequences that we designed. It may be helpful if we all meet together again to discuss this matter.

I am still very concerned about ___'s tendency to stretch the truth. It is causing her great difficulty in her relationships with other students. It is also affecting her participation in group work. It would help if you would speak with her about this.

Comments to Students

I am proud of you, ___. I know it takes courage to tell the truth sometimes.

I knew I could count on you to be honest.

I know how imaginative and creative you are, ___. But, let's remember that there is a difference between making up stories and telling the truth.

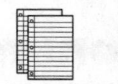

Stealing

Is Improving

Thank you for our recent meeting about ___. He is demonstrating better self-control now. I am pleased with his improvement.

___ has made an effort to be a better citizen since we last spoke. She is beginning to understand how important it is to respect the property of others. Thank you for your continued support in this area.

I am pleased with ___'s progress socially. He has demonstrated wonderful growth working with his peers and respecting their property. Thank you for reinforcing this kind of behavior at home.

Needs Improvement

I am concerned about ___'s actions in the classroom. It has come to my attention that she is taking things that do not belong to her. Let's schedule a conference at your earliest convenience to discuss this matter.

Despite our recent discussion about ___, it appears that he is continuing to take things that do not belong to him. Due to the serious nature of this problem, I think we should sit down with him and discuss this matter together. When can you meet again?

While ___ has tried to be a good citizen, she sometimes finds the property of others tempting. I know that she will work hard to improve in this area.

The issue of stealing still seems to be a problem for ___. I am concerned about this because I am sure you also want him to value honesty.

___ often finds and keeps materials and supplies that do not belong to her. Let's encourage her to return these items to the lost and found.

Comments for Students

I am so proud of you for turning in the items you found today! Honesty is a wonderful quality to have.

You know that it is wrong to take things which do not belong to you. I know you want others to be able to trust you.

It is important for all of us to know we can trust each other. I am proud of you.

Cheating

Is Improving

___ is demonstrating more confidence in his own ability. He has made great improvements in the area of independent work. Please help me continue to emphasize to ___ how important it is that he does his own work.

Since we last spoke, ___ is making a real effort to complete independent work without seeking help from her neighbors. Together, we can encourage this kind of behavior by helping her set realistic academic goals and providing the proper study conditions that will enable her to reach those goals.

___ is making good progress academically and is concentrating on doing her own work. Although there are still times when ___ looks to her neighbors for help, she is becoming an independent worker. Let's continue to stress how important it is for ___ to do her own work, especially during testing times.

Needs Improvement

The quality of ___'s work has been declining over the past few weeks. He comes to class unprepared and often relies on others to complete his work. I explained to him that this is cheating and is unacceptable; however, the problem seems to continue. Perhaps you could emphasize study habits and time management with his practice assignments at home to help him improve his classwork.

I am concerned about ___'s academic progress. Much of the independent work that she completes in class is someone else's work. Could we meet to discuss ways to raise ___'s confidence level so she is not so intimidated about doing her own work?

___'s grades have suffered this period. Unfortunately, he is still not doing his own work. I feel that I will need to separate him from the rest of the class if we cannot solve this problem. We will be taking another test this week. I'm sure that with adequate preparation, he will be able to succeed on his own.

Comments for Students

Great job on your work today! I knew you could do it all on your own!

When it is time for independent work, I am interested in your own efforts. Please do your very best without getting any help from your neighbors.

Cheating (continued)

Comments for Students
It is important to me that you understand that cheating is dishonest. You can do great work on your own. I'm counting on you to do your own work.

Sharing

Well Done
___ does a great job of sharing materials and toys with others. His classmates enjoy his company.

Is Improving
___ has made some wonderful improvements in the area of sharing classroom materials, but she still seems to have problems sharing toys at recess. I have implemented the rule with ___ that during recess, she may only play with one toy at a time. I hope this will help her get along better with others at playtime.

___ is demonstrating greater self-control with his peers during free time. He is learning how to share things and finding that it can be enjoyable to play with others. Please continue to emphasize that others can play with toys in their own way. With your support, I'm looking forward to seeing even greater progress.

I am pleased with ___'s social growth. She is finding it easier to share with others and seems to be getting along better with others. Please help me reinforce this admirable improvement.

Needs Improvement
___ is still experiencing problems with his peers. Many of these conflicts occur when ___ refuses to share materials with others. I have discussed this with him and we have agreed to use a timer when there is a toy dispute. Perhaps you could use the same strategy at home to help him learn how to share with others.

Despite our recent conference, ___ is still aggressive and bossy at playtime. Our classroom rules state that if someone puts a toy down, others are free to use it. I have spoken with ___ about this and feel that this rule really needs to be reinforced with her. Please remind her of this rule at home.

I am noticing that ___ is still having trouble sharing with others. I know that you are concerned about his peer relations and would like to see ___ understand how enjoyable it can be to play with others. Let's continue to find opportunities for him to experience the positive feelings associated with sharing.

Sharing (continued)

Comments for Students

I've noticed you are getting along well with your friends. That's wonderful!

You are doing a much better job sharing with others lately. You are a very special person, and other students enjoy playing with you. I'm proud of you.

I'm sorry that you are having trouble playing with other students at recess time. I know how much you like your friends and how much they like you. I know if you shared toys and materials more, others would be happy to play with you.

Attitude and Respect

Well Done

___'s grades are a reflection of her fine attitude toward school and authority. I know how proud you must be of her. ___ is respectful and a pleasure to have in class.

I am proud of the way ___ carries himself at school. He has a good attitude regarding academic tasks and displays respect for himself, his peers, and me.

___ is a fine student, and her attitude toward school is reflected in these outstanding grades. I am proud of the example she sets for others.

Is Improving

Although there has been some improvement in ___'s attitude, it is inconsistent. He still needs reminders that we have certain responsibilities in the classroom, lunchroom, and playground. Please help me remind him that grades are often a reflection of attitude.

___'s attitude toward others has shown improvement this grading period. However, she still seems to be careless regarding her academic work. It would help if you could discuss this matter with her and reinforce the idea that her opportunities to learn are valuable.

Thank you for your continued support with ___. He is demonstrating a better attitude toward school and his peers. However, there are still times when he is disrespectful and uncooperative. I know that ___ wants to continue to make progress. It will take frequent reminders from both of us to improve the situation.

Comments

Attitude and Respect (continued)

Is Improving

Although ___ has demonstrated a desire to get along better with others, she still needs to be reminded to express wants and needs respectfully. Thank you for continuing to work with me to suggest different ways for her to speak to others.

Our recent conference regarding ___ has been helpful. He is still exhibiting disrespectful outbursts toward me and his peers on occasion. I have spoken with ___ about his tone of voice, facial expressions, and word choice. I would appreciate it if you would speak with him again regarding this situation.

Needs Improvement

Despite our last conference with ___, she has continued to act rebelliously and disobey our classroom rules. I have explained to her that our rules are necessary to make sure that the classroom is a safe place for all students. I would like to set up another conference with you and ___ as soon as possible.

Unfortunately, ___'s attitude toward school is evident in his grades. He needs frequent reminders to follow the rules and complete his work. Please help me reinforce the rules and consequences that we set up at our last conference.

___ is capable of being a better student. Unfortunately, she does not seem to value school very much. She is careless with written work and refuses to participate in group activities. Please continue to stress the importance of education at home so that ___ can benefit from the opportunities she has at school.

Unfortunately, I have seen little improvement in ___'s attitude this grading period. His grades are suffering, and he has been disrespectful when asked to perform various tasks. I have been clear about the behavior that I expect in my classroom, and I think he understands my expectations. Perhaps you could discuss this with ___, and then we could meet for a conference with him.

I am concerned about ___'s attitude. She is frequently defiant and does not make good choices. Furthermore, she becomes angry if reprimanded in any way. I would like to set some guidelines for ___, and I think we should establish them together. When can we all meet for a conference?

Comments

Attitude and Respect (continued)

Comments for Students

Your excellent attitude is a wonderful example for the other students. You are a very special person and I enjoy having you in class.

Your hard work and respectful attitude are terrific. Thank you for being you!

I know you have been working hard to improve your attitude. It is so nice to work with you when you are positive. Keep up the good work!

Sometimes the words you choose to express your feelings are very disrespectful. We have talked about this before, and I just wanted to remind you that there are nicer ways to speak to others, even when you are unhappy.

Citizenship

Well Done

____ is a wonderful part of my class. She demonstrates respect for herself and others, as well as for our classroom rules.

I can always count on ____ to be a responsible student and a fine citizen. He is eager to help me and other students, and sets a good example by always following the school rules. I am proud of ____.

____ is a good citizen and consistently works hard to do her very best work. I have enjoyed watching her grow socially and academically.

I enjoy having ____ in class. He is a very dependable, conscientious student who is eager to volunteer for additional responsibilities.

____ is such a polite young lady! She really gets along well with others.

Is Improving

Since our last conversation, ____ has demonstrated an effort to improve. He is trying very hard to be a better citizen, but he continues to need our guidance when it comes to making good choices. I have discussed this with him, and I am sure he will focus on thinking about the effects of his actions in the future.

____ is making good progress following rules on the playground and on the bus. She still needs frequent reminders to keep her hands to herself and wait for her turn. Thank you for your continued support in these areas.

Comments

Citizenship (continued)

Is Improving

I have seen improvement in ___'s behavior lately; however, I feel he still needs our help. We have talked about positive personal qualities such as honesty, dependability, and trust. I know that ___ wants to be a better citizen.

___ has made good improvement in academic areas. She still needs to work on her behavior in the hallways, bathroom, and playground. I know you will encourage ___ to follow the rules even when a teacher isn't present.

Needs Improvement

___'s grades show good academic progress, but he is often disruptive in class and bothersome to other students after completing his work. I would like to see ___ spend his energy in more positive ways. Perhaps you could work with me to encourage him to help others after he has finished his work. I think together we can assist ___ in developing a strong leadership role in the classroom.

I have noticed that ___ is often too interested in other students' concerns. She causes problems by persuading others to engage in mischief. She needs constant supervision, and other students are beginning to avoid working with her so that they do not get into trouble. I would like to get together with you to discuss ways to help ___ learn to make better choices.

As you are aware, ___ has been reprimanded several times for failing to follow both school and classroom rules. I feel that a conference is in order, so please let me know when you are available to meet. I am sending a copy of our classroom rules for you to review with ___ before our conference.

___ does not use his time wisely in class. He would have less work to finish at home if he would concentrate on his work rather than entertaining others. I know ___ has a wonderful sense of humor, but I need your help to explain to him how inappropriate his behavior is.

I am concerned about ___. She frequently acts silly and disruptive in class. I find this to be especially true when she is unprepared. Perhaps you could make sure that ___ has her work done before school so that she is able to make valuable contributions to class discussions.

Let's encourage ___ to practice good citizenship skills like kindness, sharing, and honesty with others at home and school. Thanks for your help in this matter.

Citizenship (continued)

Comments for Students

Thank you for setting such a fine example by following the school and class-room rules. You help to make our school a great place to be!

I know you work hard to complete your assignments in class, but other students do not work as quickly as you do. Please concentrate on finding a silent activity to do while others are finishing so you do not disturb them.

I truly appreciate your classroom behavior. However, your behavior in the hallways and bathrooms is unacceptable. Maybe you could think about some ways to improve in this area.

You had a better day today. I knew you could do it! Keep up the great work.

It is important that every member of our class understands and follows our rules so that our classroom is a good place to be. I know you want to follow the rules, too. Please remember that the rules are for everyone.

Social Interaction and Skills

- ❑ Teasing, Bullying, Fighting, and Tattling
- ❑ Getting Along with Other Students
- ❑ Shyness
- ❑ Aggression
- ❑ Expressing Feelings
- ❑ Inappropriate Language
- ❑ Self-Worth

Teasing, Bullying, Fighting, and Tattling

Is Improving

Since we last spoke, ___ has made a real effort to treat others with more kind-ness. He is trying hard to interact more positively with others, but he still needs frequent reminders.

Thank you for speaking with ___ about calling other classmates names. It has always been my goal to make sure that all of my students feel good about being in my class. I think children tend to remember negative comments more vividly than positive comments. I know ___ will continue to work on this.

Comments

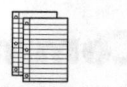

Teasing, Bullying, Fighting, and Tattling (continued)

Is Improving

Since our last conference with ___ regarding name-calling, I think that she understands that name-calling is a put-down, and will not be tolerated in our classroom. I appreciate your support in this matter.

___ tries to get along with peers, but often says hurtful things and engages in name-calling. I know that we can work together to instill in ___ how important it is to be tolerant of others.

Since we last spoke, ___ has worked hard not to engage in name-calling or to use unkind language. However, he needs to concentrate on solving conflicts on his own. ___ frequently has been tattling on others, and other students are beginning to avoid playing with him. Let's continue to help ___ look for healthy ways to resolve conflicts.

Needs Improvement

I've noticed that ___ is having difficulty with her peers. Her comments about other students can be unkind and hurtful. It is important to remember that children often perceive themselves according to how they think others view them. I have explained this to ___, but I think we need to have a conference to discuss this matter further.

___ needs constant reprimands to curtail his poor treatment of others. His peers feel uncomfortable and intimidated around ___. We need to set some clear boundaries for him and emphasize the fact that respect must be mutual. Could we set up a time for a conference?

___ is not making the kind of progress of which she is capable. I feel that poor peer relations are making her unhappy at school. Her constant confrontations often include unkind remarks and vulgar language. We need to meet to determine the cause of this behavior so we can address this problem.

Recently ___'s aggressive behavior toward others has become worse. I have explained to him that he needs to stop and think before he lashes out against other students if he doesn't get his way. I would like to schedule a conference to sit down with him together and help him develop some conflict resolution skills. He really needs our guidance in this matter.

Comments

Teasing, Bullying, Fighting, and Tattling (continued)

Needs Improvement

I am concerned about ___'s social behavior. As you know, she often gets physically aggressive toward other students. I would like to set up a conference as soon as possible so that we can meet with the school counselor to develop some strategies that will help.

___'s recent outbursts have gotten out of hand. He is fighting with other students and becoming increasingly volatile. I have explained to him that this kind of behavior will not be tolerated at school. I would like to schedule a conference as soon as possible.

___ is causing frequent disruptions in class by bullying and threatening other students. We need to meet to develop a strategy for how to solve this problem.

Comments for Students

I am proud of the way you helped your peers today! Great job!

You are a kind, helpful person to me. I know that other students would enjoy working with you if you treated them the same way. Let's try that tomorrow.

No one likes to be called names, and you know that it against our school rules. Please concentrate on being kind to others at school.

Fighting is not the way to solve problems and it will not be tolerated in our class. I know that this will not happen again. Please think of some other ways you could have handled this situation, and we can talk about it tomorrow.

You are a very bright person, and your friends like you very much. I know that you can work with your friends to resolve conflicts on your own.

Getting Along with Other Students

Well Done

___ is a wonderful student. She gets along well with others and is eager to help classmates. Many students would benefit from modeling ___'s thoughtful, generous behavior.

___ is a very thoughtful, kind classmate. Many students, both boys and girls, enjoy ___'s friendship. He has certainly made our year a pleasant one.

Comments

Getting Along with Other Students (continued)

Well Done

It is a pleasure to have ___ in class! Her hard work, ability to interact with others, and leadership skills make her a role model for other classmates.

What a treat it is to have ___ in class! His sense of humor, leadership skills, and ability to get along with everyone is to be commended.

Is Improving

___ has been making some effort to get along better with classmates, but group participation is still challenging for her. If we continue to talk with ___ about compromising and working with others to reach common goals, she will progress in this area. Thank you for your continued help with this concern.

It has truly been a pleasure watching ___ improve in the social areas we discussed at our last conference. Since we met, he has made a real effort to listen, share, and take turns. Let's continue to recognize the positive efforts ___ has made to grow in these areas.

Needs Improvement

___ continues to do well academically. However, I often see ___'s socialization skills interfering with her ability to work in the classroom, particularly in small group situations. Perhaps we should meet to discuss ways we can help ___ get along better with others by providing her with opportunities to enjoy making friends her own age.

Although ___ has many strengths, he still needs to work on getting along with others in the classroom. I am trying to invite him to join the group more and more, but his seat continues to be separated from the group. Please review with him the importance of keeping hands, feet, and all objects to himself to avoid any injuries. Let's work together on building fine socialization skills to allow ___ to feel more comfortable among his peers.

Comments for Students

Wow! You are working so hard with your group this week! I knew you could do it. Keep it up and your grades are sure to improve, too!

Three cheers for you! It's nice to see you getting along with your neighbors.

You have such wonderful ideas to share. Please try to work better with your group. You can do it!

Shyness

Is Improving

___ is making tremendous progress! What a pleasure it has been to see her opening up, sharing her ideas, and making friends. ___ continues to be somewhat quiet and timid in large group settings. I have been trying to provide class situations in which all answers are welcomed. This gives her a safe environment to respond and share her thoughts. This has opened some new doors for ___. Let's continue to encourage ___ to participate.

___ is such a sweet, quiet student. He works very hard in school each day, but seldom seems to interact with classmates. Please try to provide ___ with opportunities to interact with children his own age at home, and I will try encourage the same here at school. Perhaps with both of us working together to foster new friendships, ___ will not only find success academically, but will enjoy school socially as well, and will develop lasting friendships.

Needs Improvement

___'s smile sure brightens my day, but I would love to be able to discuss with her what makes that smile so big and bright. ___ is still painfully shy and unable to speak to anyone comfortably. We are continuing to try to make her feel safe and welcome to participate.

What a pleasure it is to have ___ in class! He is a hard worker and can sit next to any classmate and complete his tasks. However, he continues to be very shy and uncomfortable participating orally in class. ___ and I have been using a silent signal with which he shows me he knows the answer, but doesn't want to verbalize it. Perhaps we can meet to discuss ways we can make ___ feel more comfortable in group settings and willing to share answers and his clever ideas.

Comments for Students

Three cheers for you! It has been a pleasure hearing you participate in class this week. Keep up the terrific effort.

You have made great contributions to our class this week. I know you can continue to share your ideas. Great work!

You have wonderful thoughts and ideas. I would love to hear them. Let's discuss a secret signal that you can use to let me know that you are ready to share with the class. Think about it and let me know. You can do it!

Aggression

Needs Improvement

What a great helper ___ is! He sometimes helps me with errands in order to expend energy and have some time away from his desk. I have found that when his mind wanders from the task at hand, his energy often turns into altercations with classmates. Please help me to remind ___ to keep his hands, feet, and objects to himself to avoid unpleasant situations with peers. Your help and cooperation are appreciated.

___ works very hard and puts forth a great deal of effort and pride in each task with which she's presented. I have noticed, however, that this same enthusiasm often leads to aggressive behavior toward her peers. She likes to compete and often puts other's work down. I have encouraged ___ to continue to try her best and to strive to "beat" her own personal record instead of worrying about how others are doing. Perhaps you could reinforce this effort by placing a graph on the refrigerator in which ___ could visually record her progress, so we might see this aggressive, overly-competitive side less and less in the classroom.

Comments for Students

___, you have been trying extra hard this week to keep your hands to yourself, and I have noticed the improvement! I am proud of you!

___, so that your classmates will enjoy spending time with you, please try to remember our classroom rules. I know you will work harder to be your very best self.

Expressing Feelings

Well Done

___ does a wonderful job of communicating how she feels. Her facial expressions and expressive vocabulary allow us to celebrate victories with her and provide a boost when ___ is discouraged.

It is always a pleasure to see the expressions on ___'s face! He does such a good job of expressing his feelings!

Is Improving

What a pleasure ___ is to have in class! When she smiles the whole classroom brightens up! It's nice to see her feeling better about school.

Expressing Feelings (continued)

Is Improving

___ has been doing a much better job of keeping his feelings under control. Please continue reinforcing his good days!

Needs Improvement

Throughout the day children's moods can change rapidly, especially if they haven't had enough rest. Please make sure that ___ is getting enough sleep so that she can enjoy more of our day on a happy note.

___ is having a difficult time expressing his feelings. I am encouraging him to write about what bothers him. Let's schedule a conference together so that we can determine how to help ___ express his feelings more appropriately.

___ has been acting out inappropriately toward her classmates recently. I have reminded her that we need to keep our hands to ourselves even when we are upset. I would appreciate it if you could help provide ___ with some alternative actions rather than hitting when she is upset.

Comments for Students

Three cheers for you! You have really been keeping your feelings under better control this week!

It's nice to see you controlling your feelings rather than your feelings controlling you! Keep up the great work!

I know you get upset when things don't work out quite the way you had hoped. Let's get together to talk about what you can do when you get frustrated.

We all feel upset at times. Try to express your feelings using words so your classmates will better understand how you are feeling. I know you can do it!

Inappropriate Language

Needs Improvement

___ is a bright student. However, some of the language she uses throughout the day offends other classmates. Please discuss the importance of using appropriate language with ___. There will be a punishment implemented each time the problem occurs here at school.

Inappropriate Language (continued)

Needs Improvement

We have tried very hard in our classroom to establish a safe, friendly, educational environment. ___'s inappropriate language has been interfering with this positive setting and making other classmates uncomfortable. Please remind ___ to use his best manners while at school.

___ frequently uses inappropriate language in school. If this behavior continues, we will need to take further steps in reprimanding this serious offense.

Comments for Students

You have been working very hard to be a better neighbor by saying kind comments to your classmates. Thank you for an improved effort in this area!

I want you to know that I have noticed how hard you have been working at using better language in class. It's so nice to be around people who work hard and have nice things to say to others. Good work!

You are a great friend when you share nice comments with your classmates.

Sometimes the language you use makes others uncomfortable. Please remember to use your best language in class.

Self-Worth

Well Done

___ really has the confidence to try new things. How refreshing!

___ has such a wonderful feeling of self-worth, and her pride shows in all of her assignments. It is a pleasure to find the balance between being humble and motivated to expect the best of one's self. ___ has that balance.

Is Improving

___ has been feeling better about his performance, and it shows in his smile. Reviewing materials at home each evening has given ___ the confidence to participate in class.

Working together to reinforce the many wonderful things that ___ does at school has really boosted her feelings of self-worth. Thank you for your assistance. Let's continue to recognize ___'s fine qualities.

Comments

Self-Worth (continued)

Needs Improvement

I am very concerned with ___'s low self-esteem. Let's meet to discuss ways we can foster some positive experiences for ___. By working together, we can build ___'s self-worth.

___ has seemed depressed lately. I am concerned with the negative comments he has made about himself. We need to discuss ways to build a better sense of self-worth in ___. Let's work together to help him feel better about himself.

Classroom Conduct
- ❑ Absences/Make-Up Work
- ❑ Tardiness
- ❑ Classroom Behavior
- ❑ Influence on Class
- ❑ Listening/Following Directions
- ❑ Attention
- ❑ Effort
- ❑ Participation
- ❑ Cooperation

Absences/Make-Up Work

Is Improving

In fairness to ___, I have not averaged his grades at this time. I know he is working hard to complete the assignments missed during his recent illness. I will average his grades when all of his assignments have been turned in.

I am very pleased with the effort ___ has shown to maintain good attendance. Her grades reflect this effort.

___ has really been working hard to complete make-up work from his long-term illness. Your support from home to complete assignments is appreciated.

___ has been working very hard to get caught up with her work since her absence. Keep up the terrific effort.

Absences/Make-Up Work (continued)

Needs Improvement

Class participation is an important element to the success of your child in our classroom. Although it is sometimes necessary for us to be absent, ___ has missed a considerable amount of school. His absences are hindering his academic progress.

___ has missed a large number of school days. She has not completed the make-up work assigned for home review and continues to fall behind in current assignments as well. ___'s grades are reflective of the incomplete assignments and lack of effort to complete make-up work.

Because ___ has been absent from school due to a recent illness, it is impossible to average his grades at this time. Once he feels better, ___ needs to complete make-up work and turn it in. At that time, I will average his grades.

Is Improving

It is very important that your child attend school when she is well! So much learning occurs through experiments, discussion, and classroom instruction, and your child is really missing out on her education by not attending regularly.

Your child's grades reflect the lack of classroom participation due to absences.

The grades on this report card reflect ___'s incomplete assignments due to absences. It is difficult to evaluate progress without having complete assignments. Please have ___ turn in the missing assignments as soon as possible.

Comments for Students

I am happy that you are feeling better. We miss you when you are out.

Congratulations for completing all of your make-up work. I am glad you are feeling better.

Our class is not the same when you are not here to share your thoughts and ideas with us. I am glad that you are back and feeling better.

I am still missing (#) assignments from you. Please be sure to turn them in so they can be averaged into your grades. It is great to have you back!

Tardiness

Is Improving

___ is having better mornings now that she is arriving to school on time.

I have noticed an improvement now that ___ is arriving to school on time and is prepared for school each day. Thank you for your special efforts in this area.

Your efforts to wake up ___ earlier so that he has time to eat breakfast and organize materials before coming to school have had a positive effect on his school performance.

Needs Improvement

Because every minute is a valuable opportunity for your child to learn, it is important that ___ arrives to school on time each day.

Our school day begins at (time). It is important that ___ starts her day off being prepared, comfortable, and relaxed. Please help her begin each day on time.

When ___ arrives to school tardy, he often starts his day hurried, unorganized, and feeling behind and rushed. Please encourage ___ to arrive to school by (time). Arriving to school on time will allow your child a relaxed, comfortable start to each day.

Please encourage ___ to get up a little earlier to have more time for breakfast and to organize materials before arriving at school.

Comments for Students

I have noticed that you have made an effort to be here on time this week. I have enjoyed the extra time we have to talk in the morning since you have come to school earlier. Good for you!

Please try to have your books and assignments ready the night before. This will save you time in the mornings.

Classroom Behavior

Well Done

___ cooperates well with others in our classroom.

___ always demonstrates positive behavior toward learning and new activities.

Classroom Behavior (continued)

Well Done

I can always count on ___ to follow classroom rules. I am proud of the fine example that she sets for others.

___ is such a pleasure to have in class! His hard work, thoughtful ways, and sense of humor are true assets to the class.

___ is a conscientious member of our class and works hard to make positive contributions.

I am proud of the way that ___ completes tasks independently and works well with others.

___ is always kind and courteous toward others.

Is Improving

___ is working hard to improve her behavior and citizenship skills. Thank you for emphasizing our classroom rules with ___. Keep up the terrific effort.

Wow! ___ is becoming a wonderful student. He has worked hard to be thoughtful and courteous to his others, and is a good role model.

Needs Improvement

___ often displays a poor attitude towards school and learning. It would be helpful if we discuss a plan to encourage him to be more positive.

Because ___ often demonstrates inappropriate behavior, she draws negative attention from classmates with her actions.

___'s inappropriate behavior and failure to follow classroom rules often leads him to have difficulty working with groups. His grade reflects the inability to work with his group and, therefore, the inability to complete the project.

___ is a hard worker and often completes tasks independently, but she needs to work on getting along better with fellow students. Group projects are often a challenge because ___ doesn't work well with others.

___ frequently demonstrates unacceptable behavior at school. It is important for his learning and the education of the other students in the classroom that ___ refrain from disrupting the class.

Comments

Classroom Behavior (continued)

Needs Improvement

____ really needs to remember to follow our classroom rules. I have enclosed an extra copy of our rules so you can review them with ____.

Comments for Students

I certainly am proud of the way that you try so hard to be your very best self each day. Keep up the good work.

I just wanted you to know that I have noticed how hard you have been working to be a good student. I sure am glad that you are in our classroom.

Thanks for all that you do to help others in our class. We all count on you.

You are doing a much better job of following directions and using time wisely. I am proud of the improvement I see in your work.

You need to be a better neighbor in our classroom by not disturbing those around you while they are trying to finish their work. I know that you can do it.

Influence on Class

Well Done

____ is a wonderful person and a great part of my class. I can always count on him to set a good example for the other students.

____'s positive attitude toward her academic responsibilities and her friendly manner have made her a well-liked class member.

____ is a pleasant, conscientious member of my class. He is dependable, mannerly and self-confident. He has helped to make my year a pleasant one.

____ is happy and cooperative toward his academic tasks as well as his peers. He is a good student and is inspiring to others.

I can always count on ____ to be a good leader in group activities. His helpful attitude and interest in learning is a positive influence on the whole class.

____ takes an interest in our lessons and class discussions. She is agreeable and bright, and other students look forward to working with her. She has been a pleasure to have in class.

© Carson-Dellosa CD-2702   57   **Classroom Conduct**

Influence on Class (continued)

Is Improving

Thank you for your cooperation with ___. He has made wonderful improvements in all areas, including his attitude toward school. He is helpful, courteous, and sets a fine example for the other students.

I appreciate your continued cooperation with ___ this year. He has worked very hard and has made some wonderful improvements both socially and academically. Although he occasionally still makes poor choices with his peers, I have enjoyed watching his progress.

Thank you for our recent conference regarding ___ 's social skills. She works hard to be a good citizen, but often tries to influence others to break our rules. I know she wants to be a more positive influence on the class.

Needs Improvement

___ needs to work harder to be polite to others. She has a lot to offer but offends others by interrupting or not taking turns. Some work in this area would help her improve. Please help her practice these skills at home.

___ needs to think about making better choices in how he treats others. Often the tone of ___'s voice hurts other students' feelings. Many children would like to be friends with him, but this behavior gets in the way. Please talk to him about this and point out this behavior when you see it at home. If you like, I would be happy to meet with you to discuss this further.

___ needs to learn that often it is not what we say to others but how we say it that matters. She sometimes hurts others' feelings because of the way she talks to them. Please help her work on this at home. I will continue to reinforce this at school. ___ has so many positive qualities, I hate to see this get in the way!

___ often acts without thinking about others. Although I do not feel that this behavior is intentional, it does get in the way of his positive relationships with others. Please encourage ___ to take turns and share at home. These habits will help him be more successful at school.

Comments for Students.

I really appreciate your friendly attitude and the way you treat your classmates. It is a pleasure to have you in class.

Influence on Class (continued)

Comments for Students.

Thanks for sharing your great smile with all of us each day. I appreciate the way you make your classmates feel welcome and important.

You did a great job at being group leader. Your group benefitted because you were organized, kept the group on task, and involved each member in discussions. I really liked they way you divided the tasks among the group members. Congratulations on a job well done!

I wanted you to know that I noticed how you made ___ feel welcome in our class. Thanks for helping our new student learn her way around the classroom on her first day. You are one terrific kid!

I know you want to be a good example for other students. Please make sure you are doing your best and allowing others to do so by not disturbing them.

Listening/Following Directions

Well Done

___ works well in class and seems to enjoy school. I am very pleased with her ability to interpret and follow directions.

___ is a good listener in class. This enables him to follow directions and complete his work accurately.

Is Improving

___ has made wonderful improvements listening and following directions. Her grades reflect her concentration in class.

___ is anxious to please and works well in group settings. However, he sometimes does not listen and follow directions on independent work. We need to continue to remind him to be a good listener.

Although ___ is enthusiastic and eager to work, she often doesn't take time to listen to instructions or read directions. Her grades will improve if she learns to pay attention to instructions.

___ is working hard to listen to directions. Although he still finds himself rushing into assignments at times, he has made great progress in this area. Thank you for your help at home.

Listening/Following Directions (continued)

Needs Improvement

___ is a very conscientious student and is learning to follow directions well. I enjoy having her in class.

While ___ is a good student and an attentive listener, he fails to take the time to read written directions on his own. Let's encourage him to pay closer attention to directions on written work.

When ___ listens and follows directions, he is more focused and more able to complete his work correctly. You can help at home by emphasizing the directions on his practice assignments. Thank you for your continued support.

___ is a happy child and enjoys being at school. However, she is often inattentive and talkative. This makes it difficult for her to listen and pay attention to instructions. I would like to schedule a conference with you to discuss this.

When ___ listens and follows directions, he is able to complete his work accurately. This is an area on which he needs to concentrate.

Although ___ is enthusiastic and eager to work, she often does not take enough time to listen to instructions or read directions. Her grades will improve if she learns to pay attention to instructions.

Comments for Students

Congratulations! You have been doing a great job of listening and following directions. I have seen much improvement in your work.

What a great listener you are!

I like the way you have been following directions and working independently.

You need to listen to directions before you begin to work. Then, you can be sure you are doing assignments correctly.

Attention

Well Done

I can always count on ___ to be attentive in class. ___ continues to pay attention, work hard, and complete assignments.

Comments

Attention (continued)

Well Done

___ continues to pay attention, work hard, and complete assignments.

Is Improving

I am pleased to see that ___ is working so hard to pay attention in class. He has shown improvement since we last spoke. Continue to encourage him to visit with friends at appropriate times. The reward system that you started at home has made a positive impact. Thank you for your help!

I wanted to let you know that ___ has done a much better job of paying attention in class since we moved her seat. Thank you for your support in this matter. Please encourage ___ to keep up the good work.

___ has been paying better attention in class. I notice that he takes advantage of the opportunity to choose a seat himself. I am pleased that he is taking the responsibility to make choices that ensure his best work. Thank you for encouraging him to make this positive change.

Needs Improvement

___ is a great helper in class, although her conduct is affecting her academic performance. I'm sure that if she would attend to the task at hand, she could do much better.

___ seems to try hard, but he finds it challenging to focus on the current assignment and is very easily distracted. The work is becoming difficult for him, and he would benefit from daily reinforcement at home.

___ seems unable to stay focused on her work. Her attention frequently wanders; therefore, she has trouble completing the work.

___ has been steadily progressing. His greatest problem is listening attentively and keeping his mind on the task at hand. His performance will surely improve with increased concentration.

Although ___ is doing satisfactory work, I am certain she would excel if she concentrated more on her own studies instead of on her neighbors. She is very friendly and outgoing, but needs to socialize at appropriate times.

Comments

Attention (continued)

Needs Improvement

____ is a wonderful helper and always anxious to please. However, he still talks too much to his neighbors and is often inattentive. In order to improve, he needs to learn to better direct his concentration.

____ really enjoys being out of his seat to be a helper. Her independent work is usually correct, but often incomplete. She spends her time talking and distracting those around her because she is so active. ____ needs encouragement to practice better work habits.

Comments for Students

You do a great job of concentrating on your work and it shows.

I am very proud of the way that you pay attention and complete assignments.

You need to concentrate more on your work and less on what your neighbors are doing. It would make a positive difference in your grades.

It is hard for you to do your best work when visiting with neighbors. Save those conversations for the appropriate times.

Effort

Well Done

____ is to be praised for the effort she puts into her work. She can be counted on to do her best.

____'s grades reflect the effort that he puts into his work.

____ is willing to put in the time and effort to succeed. You can be proud of her. ____ always tries her best and it shows!

____ takes responsibility for doing his work in a conscientious manner. Deadlines are consistently met.

____ consistently exceeds expectations. He holds himself to a high standard of achievement and works hard to meet his goals.

____ consistently meets or exceeds expectations. His extra effort, in all that he does, is to be commended.

Effort (continued)

Well Done

It is a joy to work with ___. She pushes herself to be the best at what she does, and it shows in the quality of her work. I am very proud of her progress.

Is Improving

___ continues to display good effort in class and meets my expectations. I am impressed with his work habits.

___'s hard work pays off as reflected in her grades. She consistently does her best on a regular basis.

What a worker! ___ is someone I can count on to try to do his best.

___ is to be commended for the level of effort that she consistently puts forth. She can always be counted on to do her very best.

Needs Improvement

___'s grades, although satisfactory, are not a true indication of his capabilities. A little extra effort on his part could bring his grades up.

___'s lack of effort has negatively affected her grades for this grading period.

Lack of effort on ___'s part has resulted in lower grades. I hope to see him try harder. With a little more effort on ___'s part, his grades could be raised.

Please encourage ___ to put more effort into her homework assignments. Any extra effort would certainly be reflected in higher grades next grading period.

___'s classroom participation is good, but he needs to spend more time reviewing for tests. This extra effort would surely improve his grades next time.

___ needs to put more time and effort into checking assignments for accuracy before they are turned in.

___ seems to be satisfied with getting by with the minimum requirements. This is not a true reflection of her ability. I hope to see more effort on ___'s part in the future.

___ is happy to do the least amount of work possible to get by. With a little more effort on his part, his grades could improve.

Effort (continued)

Needs Improvement

Let's work together to encourage ___ to work harder next grading period. With a little more effort to check assignments for accuracy and reviewing for tests, her grades could be improved.

Comments for Students

You do a great job of having your work done on time. What a responsible worker you are. I am proud of you!

What a worker! I can always count on you to do your very best. Bravo!

Those C's could be B's with a little more effort on your part. Go for it!!

Participation

Well Done

I can always count on ___ to enhance classroom discussions with his comments, thoughts, and insights.

___ participates regularly in class discussions.

Our class appreciates the way that ___ shares her thoughts and ideas during class discussions. ___'s comments are appropriate and relate to the topic.

What a delight ___ is to have in class! He shares his knowledge and experiences during class discussions.

___ regularly contributes in class by sharing her knowledge and experiences. This adds to our class discussions.

___ is a great thinker! I enjoy how she shares her ideas in class. Her participation enhances lessons for all of us.

___ expresses ideas in class with confidence. I welcome his participation.

Is Improving

___'s grades reflect the effort she has made to participate in class. She shares experiences and ideas regularly. Thank you for encouraging her to do so.

Comments

Participation (continued)

Is Improving

I am really pleased with the effort I have seen ___ make to participate in class. His confidence in his thoughts and ideas is growing daily. How lucky we are to hear what ___ has to say.

I am so proud of the way ___ has blossomed! She participates regularly in class. Her confidence grows as she sees the positive reaction other students have to her comments. Please encourage ___ to keep up the good work.

Although participating in class continues to be an area of difficulty for ___, he is to be commended for the effort that he has made to do so. I think this is a skill that will improve with practice. Please continue to encourage him at home. Your help is important and very much appreciated.

Needs Improvement

___ is reluctant to share ideas in class. Her participation would be welcomed by all of us.

I feel that ___ has great thoughts and ideas but is afraid to share them in class. Please encourage ___ to share his ideas in class.

Class participation is an area of weakness for ___. Please encourage her to share her thoughts and ideas in class.

___ could bring up his grades if he participated in class more often. His ideas are important to the class, and participation is a part of his grade.

___ knows the correct answer when called upon, but rarely volunteers to answer questions in class. Let's work together to improve this area of performance by encouraging her to share at least two ideas or thoughts per day.

Our class would benefit from contributions by ___ during class discussions. Please help me encourage him to share thoughts in class.

___'s grade has suffered because of her lack of class participation. Her written work shows that she knows the material. The next step is having her share her knowledge with others in class. I know she can do it!

Comments for Students

I can count on you to share your thoughts and ideas with the class. Thanks!

Comments

Participation (continued)

Comments for Students

You make our classes more interesting by sharing your thoughts and ideas.

What a great thinker you are. Thanks for sharing your ideas with us!

You have such great thoughts and ideas. I wish that you would share them with us more often during class discussions.

I know you often know the right answer. I hope you will raise your hand more.

Cooperation

Well Done

It is a pleasure to have ___ in class. His cooperation is appreciated by classmates.

___ is easy to work with. Her cooperative attitude makes her a sought-after group member.

I appreciate the way that ___ works with others. He can be counted on to lend a helping hand. He is cooperative and willing to work towards classroom goals.

It is obvious that ___ enjoys school. She is happy and cooperative. Her fine grades are a reflection of a wonderful attitude toward responsibility.

Is Improving

___ has made great strides in working with others. This improvement in his attitude is appreciated.

___ has really made an effort to cooperate with others. I have seen much growth in the way that she works with others. Her cooperation is appreciated.

I appreciate the way that ___ has made an effort to work well with others. Taking turns and listening has helped him to be a more cooperative classmate.

___ has shown great improvement and is cooperating with others. I feel that giving him the additional classroom responsibilities with others has helped. It is important that you and I continue to reinforce this kind of behavior.

___ is very conscientious and very aware of her grades. We need to remind her to cooperate with others in group work so everyone can participate and learn.

Comments

Cooperation (continued)

Needs Improvement

I am concerned about ___'s attitude. He is often uncooperative. Please talk to him about taking turns, sharing, and listening to others. This would help him develop a more cooperative attitude.

I hope to see an improvement in the way ___ works with others. She is often uncooperative and argumentative. This gets in the way of her relationships with others. Please help me monitor this behavior and encourage improvement.

___ often displays an unwillingness to work with others. He can be argumentative and uncooperative, which adversely affects his group grades. Please talk to him about being more cooperative. I look forward to seeing a positive change.

___ does well on independent work and completes homework assignments regularly. However, she experiences frequent problems with peers. Together, we need to impress upon ___ that she has a responsibility to get along with others and do her best to be part of our team.

___ continues to get into trouble with other children in the classroom and on the playground. I have spoken with ___ about being cooperative and helping other students. Let's emphasize ___'s strengths so that he feels more confident and willing to work with others.

Comments for Students

Congratulations! You are such a team player. I have seen improvement in the way that you cooperate and work with others. Keep it up!

I am pleased to see how hard you are trying to do a better job of listening to others' ideas. You have really improved by taking turns and arguing less.

I really like the way that you helped your classmate yesterday. How kind of you to make sure that she understood what to do. Keep up the good work.

I know you want your group to do well, but you need to remember that no one in the group is the boss. You all need to work together to make decisions.

You really seem to know the material from today well. Perhaps tomorrow you could help the others in your group more so that they can learn it also.

Academic Performance

Classwork
- ❏ Work Completed in Class
- ❏ Demonstrating an Interest in Learning
- ❏ Quality of Work
- ❏ Using Time Effectively
- ❏ Completing Work Fully and on Time

Work Completed in Class

Well Done

___ takes an interest in her work and is cooperative and hardworking. This is obvious by her outstanding progress. I truly enjoy having ___ in my class.

___ is very dependable and a model student. He enjoys taking an active role in our classroom activities. His excellent work is a reflection of his effort and positive attitude.

I am pleased about the advances ___ has made in her classwork. She is a conscientious child and her hard work is paying off.

___ is a responsible student with a positive attitude. He puts forth good effort and shows pride in his work. He continues to do outstanding academic work.

I am very proud of ___'s progress. She takes an active role in her learning and has shown growth in all subject areas.

Because ___ has increased his efforts on assignments, his grades have really improved. I am proud of ___'s hard work and responsible attitude.

___ has been working hard on her classwork and it shows! Good for her!

Thank you for taking time out of your busy day to read to ___!

___ is a great problem solver. His creative thinking skills are working overtime, and it is reflected in his grades.

Comments

Work Completed in Class (continued)

Well Done

Your daughter can recall all fifty of our state capitals!

Reading skills are certainly a strength of ___'s. He can always be found with a book in his hand.

Is Improving

I am delighted with ___'s improvements. Let's continue to encourage her to concentrate on assignments and put forth her best efforts.

___ should be commended for his recent successes. I am proud of his efforts to improve his grades. ___'s hard work is paying off!

___ is learning to complete assignments fully and on time. Her grades are improving. Thank you for your cooperation. Let's continue working together!

Now that ___ is completing his assignments correctly and on time, let's concentrate on helping him choose more worthwhile free time activities, such as reading a library book, working on the computer, or reviewing skills.

___ is an excellent reader and recalls information beautifully. Let's encourage her to read aloud to practice her fluency.

___ is such a wonderful author. His strengths are (subject) and (subject) when writing stories/letters/paragraphs. He can improve by focusing on (subject).

Needs Improvement

___ continues to put forth effort and show responsibility. However, the work is difficult for her. She needs extra practice at home to grasp some concepts.

___ is struggling with grade level assignments. Although he has a positive attitude and tries hard, ___ fails to grasp many concepts. When are you available for a conference?

___ tries hard, but has difficulties in all areas. She needs extra practice at home. Let's get together so we can establish a home study program.

___'s lack of progress concerns me. He is not working to his potential and has a general lack of interest in school. He needs constant encouragement to stay on task and complete assignments. Please contact me for a conference.

Work Completed in Class (continued)

Needs Improvement

___ still struggles with independent work due to poor reading skills and often relies on neighbors for help. Extra time spent reading at home would help.

Comments for Students

I like the way you are trying so hard to bring up your grades. Your hard work and dedication will pay off.

Congratulations on terrific grades! I can tell you're working hard. Way to go!

Let's keep working together to improve these grades. I know you can do it!

I know that (subject) is hard for you, but with some extra time spent studying at home, your grade will get better.

___, make sure that you ask for help when you do not understand an assignment. I am always happy to help you learn.

Demonstrating an Interest in Learning

Well Done

___ is a hard working student and demonstrates a real desire to learn.

___ is a good student. His fine attitude and interest to learn set a wonderful example for the other students in the class.

Is Improving

___ is making great progress. The students in our class have enjoyed extending their learning through the different things ___ has brought to share with them.

I am delighted with the progress ___ has made this grading period. She has really demonstrated an interest in our current units of study and has extended that learning independently. She is a pleasure to have in class.

Needs Improvement

___ certainly enjoys drawing and artistic activities. Unfortunately, he spends much time on these kinds of endeavors when he should be working on class material. Maybe ___ could work on some special in-class art activities that relate to our current unit of study.

Demonstrating an Interest in Learning (continued)

Comments for Students

What a great job you did on sharing with our class. We all learned something new thanks to you.

You have worked very hard on our unit. I especially like the effort you made to share with us.

You are quite the expert! Thanks for sharing your project with all of us.

Quality of Work

Well Done

____ is a responsible student and a hard worker. She takes great pride in her work and always does a neat job. She has a cooperative attitude and takes an active role in her learning.

____ is showing steady improvement in basic skills and readily assumes responsibilities. It is obvious that he takes pride in completing his work correctly and neatly.

Is Improving

I am very pleased with the improvement I see in ____'s work. Her efforts to improve have paid off!

Thanks for helping to check ____'s work for accuracy and neatness. I have noticed positive progress in these areas.

____ is to be praised for the improvement he shows in the quality of his work.

____ is showing steady improvement in the quality of her assignments and readily assumes academic responsibilities. It is obvious that she is beginning to take pride in completing her work correctly and neatly.

Needs Improvement

____ is showing good growth in the basic skills. However, I am concerned that the quality of his work is not what it could be. His work tends to be messy and appears hurried. He needs frequent reminders to slow down and take pride in every assignment he completes.

Comments

Quality of Work (continued)

Needs Improvement

____ is progressing well, although her written work is not what it could be. She needs to improve the quality of her work by focusing on the neatness and accuracy of assignments.

____ is completing all his independent work, but often it is done in such a hurry that it is incorrect. You can see by his current grades that he needs encouragement to slow down and work more carefully.

____ is struggling because she makes many careless errors. We need to continue to provide guidance so she will take the time to check her work.

____ shows satisfactory progress. However, he tends to complete his assignments too quickly, which leads to poor written work and careless errors.

Comments for Students

Congratulations for a job well done! You have made a very good effort to check your work for accuracy and to improve the neatness of your assignments. Keep up the good work.

You do a great job of checking your work. Good for you!

It is very difficult to read your work. You need to slow down and improve the neatness of your work.

You need to check your assignments before you turn them in. Taking a few extra minutes to check your assignments would pay off in higher grades.

Using Time Effectively

Well Done

____ completes all assignments and has a positive attitude toward learning.

I am proud of the way ____ works. She uses time efficiently to complete her work accurately.

____ is to be commended for working independently. He uses class time wisely by starting homework assignments.

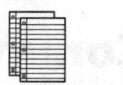

Using Time Effectively (continued)

Well Done

___ does a great job of focusing on the task at hand and making good use of her time.

Is Improving

___ continues to work throughout our class time; however, he still requires frequent reminders to stay on task.

Although ___ needs to continue to focus on using her time effectively, she is showing improvement.

___ has done a nice job of using his time more wisely. I see improvement in the quality of ___'s assignments. He is meeting deadlines in a more timely fashion.

Needs Improvement

___ is really showing improvement in her classwork. However, she needs help in other areas. She often talks to neighbors and is easily distracted from her work. If she used her work time more wisely, she would surely do better.

___ is very responsible in his duties as classroom helper, but he continues to rush through his work and then distracts neighbors by talking or wandering around the room. As a result, his work is suffering.

___ wastes too much time preparing to work. She needs to put more effort into completing her assignments.

___ is capable of doing better work. He does not use his class time wisely. He needs to remember that there are designated times for play and for work.

Comments for Students

Three cheers for you for using your time wisely! It's nice to have less work to take home.

You would have less homework if you took advantage of your time to work independently.

If you used your class time wisely, you would have less homework. Why don't you try it?

Using Time Effectively (continued)

Comments for Students

Please be considerate of your time and that of your neighbors. Visiting with friends during class causes you to take home more work.

You need to do a better job of having materials prepared before each class.

You would have less homework each night if you finished your independent work in class.

Completing Work Fully and On Time

Well Done

___ can always be counted on to have his work completed and turned in on time. I am very proud of the responsibility that he shows in this area.

___ is to be commended for the way that she assumes responsibility for having assignments completed and ready to turn in on time. Her grades reflect the effort that she puts forth.

I am very proud of the way that ___ meets deadlines. I can count on him to have assignments completed and accurately done.

What a responsible student ___ is! She consistently makes the effort to have completed assignments turned in on time.

___ is a responsible and conscientious student. Assignments are completed and consistently turned in on time.

Is Improving

I am very proud of the improvement that ___ has made in having his assignments completed in a timely fashion. Thanks for your help and support.

___'s grades have improved because of the effort that she has made to have assignments completed and turned in on time. I am confident that this effort will continue.

What a great job ___ did to improve this grading period! Completing assignments and turning them in on time made a big difference in his grade. Let's continue to encourage him to keep up the good work. Your help and support is appreciated.

Comments

Completing Work Fully and On Time (continued)

Is Improving
___ has really done a good job in taking responsibility for completing assignments and meeting deadlines. Her grades have improved because of her efforts in these areas.

Needs Improvement
___'s grades are suffering because assignments are not completed and turned in on time. A little effort to improve in these areas would result in better grades. Let's encourage ___ to work harder this grading period to be more responsible.

___ is not showing responsibility for completing work and meeting deadlines. I feel that he knows the concepts that have been taught, but missing and incomplete assignments are lowering his grades. Let's encourage him to put forth more effort this grading period.

Missing and incomplete assignments are having a negative effect on ___'s grades. A little more effort on her part could turn this around.

___ needs to assume more responsibility for getting assignments completed and turned in on time.

___ continues to turn in incomplete or late work. Please let me know of a convenient time for you to come in to discuss this with me. Perhaps we could think of a way that we can work together to bring about a positive change.

I continue to be concerned about the number of late and incomplete assignments ___ has. Often his work is turned in incomplete or is not turned in at all. More responsibility on ___'s part would make a big difference in his grades.

Comments for Students
What a responsible student you are! I can always count on you to complete your work and see that it is turned in on time. Three cheers for you!

Completing assignments and meeting deadlines are two very important study habits. These are areas of strength for you. Congratulations on a job well done!

Congratulations for turning in all your assignments on time. Your grade reflects the effort that you make in this area. Keep up the good work!

Classwork

Comments

Completing Work Fully and On Time (continued)

Comments for Students

I am very proud of the effort you made this grading period to see that your assignments were completed and turned in on time. Your grades have improved because of the effort that you made. Keep up the good work.

Congratulations on a job well done. Your grades are better because of the effort that you made to complete assignments on time. Keep up the good work.

Congratulations! Your hard work is paying off. I'm sure we'll continue to see your grades improve as you complete and turn in your assignments on time.

Well done! Your efforts to complete assignments and turn them in on time has made a big difference in your grades. I am so proud of you. Excellent work!

Work Completed Outside of Class
- ❑ Assignment Folder
- ❑ Homework
- ❑ Study Habits

Assignment Folder

Well Done

___ is a serious student and works hard to meet expectations. He has learned to utilize his assignment sheet and folder to stay organized. Thank you for continuing to check his folder and helping him improve his organizational skills.

I enjoy having ___ in class. I am very pleased with the way ___ has learned to use the assignment folder correctly. This has really improved her organization.

Is Improving

___ is assuming more responsibility for his work. He still needs to concentrate on maintaining he assignment folder in order to strengthen his organizational skills. Thank you for your continued support.

There has been a noticeable improvement in ___'s homework completion. Although there are still times when she has forgotten that an assignment is due, I know that she will be able to continue to improve if she utilizes the assignment folder and writes her assignments on the assignment sheet.

Assignment Folder (continued)

Needs Improvement

Thank you for our recent conference. As we discussed, ___ needs to remember to write his assignments down on the assignment sheet and to organize his work in the folder. I am sure that if he concentrates on this, ___ will be able to complete his practice assignments.

___ is a very active child and sometimes finds it difficult to follow the routine in our room. I know that if ___ assumes the responsibility of taking the time to use the assignment folder correctly, her practice work will improve.

___ works hard to complete her assignments. However, she has trouble finding them when she gets to school. I would suggest that ___ use just one folder in which to organize her work. This will help her keep track of her materials.

Although ___ is eager to participate in class discussions, she often gets behind when her homework is not prepared. I would like to see her continue to make valuable contributions to our discussions by completing her assignments on time. Proper use of the assignment folder will assist her greatly in this.

___'s homework is often incomplete or missing. I know that ___ wants to be prepared for class. Perhaps both you and I could check his assignment sheet daily to ensure that all assignments are being written down and his work is organized in the folder. Could we meet to discuss this?

Comments for Students

I am very proud of the way you use your assignment folder to keep your work organized. You do a super job!

Congratulations! You are trying hard to use your assignment folder to keep track of assignments. Your work has improved greatly! Keep it up.

Please make more of an effort to copy assignments onto your assignment sheet so that you know what needs to be done while you are at home.

You need to bring your assignment folder to each class. It is important to copy assignments and organize your work. You can do it!

Be sure to regularly clean out your assignment folder so that you are not confused by old papers.

Comments

Homework

Well Done

____ is a conscientious and cooperative student. He has completed all home-work assignments and is well-prepared for class discussions, quizzes, and tests. I am proud of his efforts.

____ displays a great sense of responsibility. She completes both in-class inde-pendent tasks and homework assignments completely and accurately. I enjoy having such a dependable student in class.

____ is a dependable and hardworking student. His outstanding test scores result from daily preparation and returning quality homework.

Is Improving

Thank you for your interest in and help with ____'s work. ____ is continuing to turn in completed homework assignments. I am happy to see this improvement. Let's continue our daily communication.

I'm pleased that ____ is returning homework assignments more consistently. He is better prepared for class lately and participates in class discussions.

____'s grades are improving. Her effort to complete homework assignments is the major cause. Let's continue to encourage this sense of responsibility.

I'm proud of the improvement in ____'s work habits. Since our last conference, he has made an effort to turn in assignments that are correct and complete.

Thank you for providing ____ with a consistent time and place to study at home. She is now returning completed assignments.

Needs Improvement

____ needs to develop a better sense of responsibility. His homework is often incomplete or missing. Let's work together on a plan to improve this behavior.

The decline in ____'s grades is due to poor test grades and inadequate home-work assignments. She is unprepared for class and unable to contribute. I would like a conference at your earliest convenience.

____ fails to finish independent assignments at home. He has several incomplete homework assignments this grading period. I think a homework contract is in order. Please contact me.

Homework (continued)

Needs Improvement

___ is not returning homework assignments. She often forgets or says there is no time. She needs a consistent time and place for studying at home.

Comments for Students

You have turned in all your homework! Outstanding! I know I can always count on you!

Congratulations on returning all your homework assignments! Three cheers for a job well done!

Thank you for doing a better job returning your homework. I love to see such fantastic improvements.

I know that with a little more effort you could finish your homework assignments. Let's give it a try. I know you can do it.

Study Habits

Well Done

___ does an excellent job preparing for tests and quizzes. I appreciate this conscientious attitude.

I'm proud of the hard work ___ is doing. He is well prepared for class and makes positive contributions.

Using good study habits is an important skill to learn. It's nice to see ___ practicing these habits.

Terrific! We can all learn good time management skills by watching ___ find challenging activities to do when her work is complete.

Is Improving

Since we established a daily study time and place, I've seen a marked improvement in ___'s assignments and class participation. Let's continue to praise him for his efforts.

___ is doing a better job of getting started on tasks. She wastes less time preparing and more time working quietly.

Study Habits (continued)

Is Improving

___ is working hard to concentrate on assignments instead of on his neighbors. Let's continue to encourage this behavior.

Needs Improvement

___ is often unprepared for tests and quizzes. He needs a consistent study time and daily review.

___ normally does good work, but several times her assignments have been incomplete because she enjoys talking to neighbors instead of working quietly. Let's work together to encourage good study habits.

___ has been acting silly. Instead of working independently, he is joking with peers. His work is suffering. ___ needs to learn that work time is serious.

___ often comes to class unprepared for discussions because she doesn't know the material. Please help me establish daily study habits instead of waiting until the night before the test to prepare.

___ generally works hard and has a positive attitude. However, during work time he often talks excessively instead of concentrating on work. His grades would improve if he focused on the task at hand.

___ is cooperative and courteous, but requires a lot of attention and supervision from me during independent work time. He seems more interested in art projects and note writing. Please contact me so we can discuss how to help ___ develop better study habits.

During work time, ___ often talks loudly and bothers her neighbors. Let's have a conference to discuss ways to improve her study habits.

Comments for Students

I love the good grades you're getting on tests and quizzes. Your hard work is really paying off! Bravo!

I'm proud of your efforts to spend more time studying and less time talking. I knew you could do it!

Let's try to work more and talk less during class time. You and your neighbors would both get a lot more accomplished.

Comments

Study Habits (continued)

Comments for Students

You would have a lot less homework if you studied more during work time.
Let's give it a try.

Organization and Preparedness

- ❑ Organizational Skills
- ❑ Materials
- ❑ Desk and Locker or Cubbie

Organizational Skills

Well Done

I'm proud of the organizational skills ___ has developed! He is always ready
with materials and never fails to turn in completed assignments!

___ has excellent organizational skills. Because she is so prepared for class, she
is able to contribute successfully.

___ is a conscientious and attentive student. He has developed outstanding
organizational skills. Being so organized allows him to focus his energies on
the important tasks at school!

Being prepared and organized are just a few of the good qualities I find in ___.

Is Improving

I appreciate ___'s efforts to keep his materials and desk organized. He is better
prepared when class begins and is more consistent returning assignments.

Thank you for your cooperation. ___ is better organized now that we help her
monitor papers in her folder. With a bit more guidance, she will be able to do
this on her own.

I'm happy to see ___ developing a sense of responsibility and organization.
Assignments are not only being completed, but they are being turned in on
time! He is doing a much better job filing and retrieving papers.

I've noticed an improvement in ___'s ability to stay on task and turn in completed work. Without such a cluttered work space, she is better able to concentrate on the importance of assignments.

Organizational Skills (continued)

Is Improving

I'm delighted to see ___ developing a sense of organization and timeliness. Papers are being returned and filed away properly. Using just one work folder certainly has helped!

Needs Improvement

___ needs to develop better organizational skills. He has difficulty finding materials and getting important messages and papers home. I suggest we begin a daily checking system to help monitor his organization.

___ is quite inconsistent in returning in-class assignments. The problem is not in completing the work, but rather in turning it in. Her work space is very cluttered and unorganized, and she has trouble locating papers. Keeping a tidy cubbie and using just one folder would help.

___ needs help getting and staying organized. He is unable to find materials when needed because he has so many extra items on his locker. Let's begin by taking home all unnecessary items, using just one folder for home-school papers, and monitoring that folder.

I am concerned about ___. Papers are not being turned in, and she is not ready for class on time. In order to help her develop organizational skills, let's get together to discuss a daily contract.

___ has had difficulty focusing on work lately. He is distracted by all the materials in his desk and is unable to concentrate on assignments.

When it is time to prepare to go home, ___ seems lost. She isn't sure what goes home for homework, what needs to be turned in, and where to put any of it. I'd like to start using an assignment sheet or contract to guide ___'s organization.

Comments for Students

You are so well prepared for class! I appreciate your thoughtful contributions!

Bravo for always being so organized and keeping track of your things. You are a great example for our class.

You are so much more organized now that you only use one work folder. Isn't it a lot easier to find homework and put away paper? I knew you could do it.

Organizational Skills (continued)

Comments for Students

Thank you for being a much better messenger and making sure important papers make it home! I'm glad I can count on you.

I can see that you are having trouble turning in assignments and staying organized. Let's talk about using a homework contract/assignment folder.

Be sure to set your alarm so that you have plenty of time for breakfast and getting an organized start to your day.

You may want to allow yourself more time each morning to get organized and check your materials before coming to school. You can do it!

Materials

Well Done

___ consistently has the supplies and materials that he needs to do his work. Thank you for your support.

___ always has the materials and supplies that she needs to complete her assignments. This positive habits enables ___ to make the most of the time she has to work in class.

I appreciate the way that ___ checks to be sure that he has the materials and supplies he needs to do his class assignments. What a great habit to develop!

Is Improving

___ has shown improvement now that she has the proper materials to complete tasks at school. Thank you for your help.

Thank you for your cooperation and support for getting ___ the materials needed for school.

___ has had excellent productivity now that she has the materials to complete school tasks.

Needs Improvement

___ often arrives unprepared for class. Please be sure he has the proper materials to bring to class. Thank you in advance for your cooperation and support!

Comments

Materials (continued)

Needs Improvement

In order for ___ to get the complete benefit from school, she needs to have appropriate materials each day. She often does not have several items. It would be helpful if you could assist her in getting these items and sending them to school with her tomorrow.

___ brings inappropriate materials to school and frequently plays with these items during important instructional time. Please help ___ get organized for school and monitor the items being brought to school. Your assistance is appreciated!

Comments for Students

Please make sure that you have your materials on hand and are ready to work. Using class time wisely will cut down on the work you need to take home.

Please be sure to sharpen your pencils each morning when you come to school.

Please bring the correct books and materials to each class. This will help you be ready to work right away.

Desk and Locker or Cubbie

Is Improving

I'm happy to see ___'s effort to take papers home and keep a clean locker. He is better prepared for class and can find materials much more easily.

I've seen a big improvement in ___'s organization since we cleaned out her cubbie. With an uncluttered space, she is better able to locate important papers and books.

Despite our encouragement, ___ still has a tendency to pack his locker full of papers and trash. Let's implement a daily locker and bookbag check until this behavior is back on track.

Excellent! I'm proud of the way ___ does a better job of keeping her desk organized.

Comments

Desk and Locker or Cubbie (continued)

Needs Improvement

___ has trouble getting organized for class. Keeping a tidy locker with a minimum of folders would help him. With less clutter in the locker, it would be easier to file and retrieve papers.

I'm sending home a stack of old graded papers with ___ today. We cleaned out our desks, and hers contained these old assignments, some of which had never been turned in. Let's begin a daily check of ___'s folder to make sure that papers are coming home.

___ has been keeping old papers in his locker. I will implement a periodic locker check, and I'd like you to encourage him to bring assignments home.

___ has been saving old uneaten lunches in her cubbie. Let's work together to make sure leftovers go in the trash or go home.

___ needs help getting and staying organized. He is unable to find materials when needed because he has so many extra items on his desk. Let's begin by taking home all unnecessary items, using just one folder for home-school papers, and monitoring that folder.

___ has had difficulty focusing on work lately. He is distracted by all the materials in his cubbie and cannot concentrate on his work. Please make sure that ___ brings only appropriate materials to school.

Comments for Students

I love the way your desk always looks so neat and clean. You set a great example for the rest of the class!

Thank you for making the effort to clean out your desk and keep it clean. It makes it easier to find things, doesn't it? Great job!

You've been having trouble lately being prepared for class and finding your materials. Why don't we find some time before or after class or during recess to clean out your desk? That will make your job a lot easier.

Special Situations

Personal Issues
- ❏ Clothing
- ❏ Lice
- ❏ Hygiene
- ❏ Tissues
- ❏ Restroom Use

Clothing

Well Done

___ always looks so refreshed and ready to start her day. Thank you for making a neat, clean appearance a top priority.

___ comes to school always looking his very best. Thank you for sending ___ dressed for success.

Is Improving

___ is looking so much more confident, refreshed, and ready for each new day! This new confidence overflows into her social skills and willingness to participate in class as well. She certainly has been working to improve the clothing issues discussed at our last conference. Your assistance in this area is appreciated. Let's continue to reinforce the cleanliness and neatness at school and home.

___ always looks nice but has been complaining of getting too hot/cold throughout the school day. We try to go outside each day when the weather permits. Your assistance with sending ___ to school in appropriate dress would be greatly appreciated and will make him more comfortable throughout the day.

Needs Improvement

Although ___ often comes to school with a bright smile, I often have to remind her of our dress code. Please review our school's policy with ___. I will be happy to answer any questions you may have regarding this policy established by the board of education. Your assistance is appreciated.

Clothing (continued)

Needs Improvement

____ has been dressing in outfits that do not meet our school's policy on appropriate dress. Understanding that children like to demonstrate their individual personalities by the way they dress, we still need to encourage ____ to do so while not offending others. Please refer to our school's handbook regarding the dress code and review it with your child. Your assistance is appreciated.

Comments for Students

Wow! I am proud of the way you have been arriving to school lately. You look ready to learn and eager to give your very best.

Nice job, ____! You certainly have been coming to school dressed for success.

I would like to see you be more comfortable at school. Please try to dress appropriately for hot/cold weather.

When choosing clothes for school, try to remember that we have certain rules about what is appropriate to wear.

Lice

Improving

Thank you for your continued help and support in treating ____'s hair for head lice. Her condition has certainly been improving and only a few nits remain in her hair. ____'s attitude has improved now that she has been in school and able to participate in classroom discussions and group projects. Let's continue to check regularly and treat ____'s hair, bedding, and laundry as needed so the problem does not recur. Your time, effort, and cooperation are appreciated!

Needs Improvement

____ has been working hard when he is in school. However, due to the absences he has had recently, his grades do not reflect ____'s best work. I have enclosed information to assist you in proper treatment for head lice. Please contact me if you have questions or if I can be of further assistance.

____ is such a sweet student. She is always eager to help out in the classroom. Unfortunately, due to the fact that she continues to have head lice, she doesn't get to socialize with classmates as often as she needs. Let's work together to help ____ remain in school.

Comments

Lice (continued)

Needs Improvement

____ continues to have lice and needs to remain separated from classmates until the condition is under control. Please check ____'s hair regularly at home and treat as needed. As our school policy states, we will continue to check for head lice at school and separate students who carry them. Our school nurse is available to assist you if you need materials to read regarding proper treatment or products to combat this condition. Thank you for your help and cooperation.

Comments for Students

It is so nice having you back in school with us! You must feel better, too. Keep up the good work!

Let's find some time in our day to visit the school nurse. Maybe she can give us some information and materials to help you stop itching.

Hygiene

Needs Improvement

____ always has such a bright smile. Let's encourage him to keep it looking nice by reminding him to brush his teeth regularly each day.

To keep ____'s beautiful smile, let's both take a few minutes each day to remind her to take good care of her teeth by brushing and flossing regularly. Perhaps in working together, ____ will see the importance and make good dental health habits a priority.

All children grow and mature at different rates. Along with this new transition in life many changes begin to occur. Our children turn to us, teachers and parents, for guidance about personal hygiene skills which may save them some embarrassment among their peers. Perhaps we should meet to discuss how we can introduce new hygiene skills in an appropriate manner with ____.

Comments for Students

Your smile sure brightens my day! Remember to brush your teeth twice a day to keep that beautiful smile!

____, to make sure you always have such a beautiful smile, remember to brush your teeth twice a day. You can do it!

Hygiene (continued)

Comments for Students

Let's visit the school nurse to get some ideas about why your teeth are bothering you.

Tissues

Needs Improvement

___ seems to have terrible luck and continuously catches those nasty cold symptoms. Please encourage ___ to come to school prepared with a pocket full of tissues. Perhaps if we both encourage ___ to wash his hands he will be able to dodge those germs.

___ is often sneezing and frequently seems to have a runny nose. Has the possibility of allergies been discussed? Let me know if there is something we can do in the classroom to make ___ more comfortable and "sneeze-free". Perhaps you could encourage ___ to bring in a small box of tissues to keep at her desk to make it easier for her to manage her sneezing.

___ seems to have caught a cold, as many of us do this time of the year, and could use a box of tissues to help get him through the "runny nose stage," Let's both try to remind ___ to wash his hands frequently to avoid spreading germs.

Comments for Students

Please bring a box of tissues to keep at your desk until your cold symptoms are gone. I hope you feel better soon!

Having a cold and a runny nose is never fun. Be sure to carry a few extra tissues in your pocket. It will help you to have tissues available when you need one. Try it and see!

Please wash your hands more often to keep from spreading those germs. You will feel better in no time!

Restroom Use

Needs Improvement

In our school, we try to encourage our students to become more independent. ___ seems to have difficulty when asked to use the restroom. Quite often, she disturbs the other students who are using the facility at the same time. Please review proper restroom etiquette with ___ at home.

Comments

Restroom Use (continued)

Needs Improvement
___ is still having accidents in the classroom. Let's work together to reward ___ for attempting to use the restroom on a schedule even before he may feel the need.

Comments for Students
You have been working very hard to be a better citizen and I appreciate your efforts! Thank you for respecting your classmates' privacy in the restroom.

I know bathroom behavior has been a problem for you, but I am counting on you to remember the rules we have discussed.

Miscellaneous
- ❑ Sick Child
- ❑ New Child
- ❑ Moving Child
- ❑ End of School Year
- ❑ Unpaid Fees

Sick Child

I am so sorry to hear that ___ is in the hospital. I would like to visit when she feels up to it. Please let me know if that would be okay. I will save her assignments, but let's not worry about homework until ___ is back to her old self.

Our class misses ___ and would like to do something to cheer him up while he is in the hospital. Would it be okay for me to visit or would you rather I make arrangements to send a gift to you? Please do not worry about assignments until ___ is up to it. His health comes first.

We all miss ___. It is not the same in our room without her smile. I will keep track of assignments but please do not worry about those until she is up and around. A tutor may be available to help. When would be a convenient time for me to call to see how ___ is doing?

Sick Child (continued)

Comments for Students

I am so sorry that you are not feeling well. Our class is not the same without you. Rest and take care of yourself so that you will soon be back with us!

It is lonesome without you! We all miss your smile and the good ideas that you share. Take good care of yourself, and you will be back with us in no time.

I was happy to hear that you are doing better. We miss you very much and hope that you will soon be back to brighten up our room. I will call you next week to see how you are doing.

Your parents have been telling me how brave you have been during your hospital stay. I am very proud of you! I know that is tough to be sick, but continue to follow the doctor's orders and you will soon be good as new. We sure miss you! Things are not the same without you!

New Child

___ is a welcome addition to our class. I think that he is making a good adjustment. He has many friends already and fits in perfectly! Please feel free to call if you have questions or concerns.

___ is very nice and I am happy to have her in my class. She seems a little shy and uncertain at times, so I have assigned a buddy to help her get acquainted with other classmates and to help her find her way around our building. I think that this will help. Don't hesitate to let me know if you have questions. I would be happy to meet with you if you have concerns.

___ continues to have problems adjusting to our classroom. Although she has been here for several weeks, she does not follow classroom rules or procedures. I would like to meet with you to discuss ways that we can work together to make ___'s time at school more productive.

I am concerned that ___ is struggling in math. It appears that we are further ahead in learning math facts than he was at his previous school. I am sending home some extra practice papers and a set of flash cards. Please work with ___ for 10-15 minutes per night to help him catch up. I would be happy to speak with ___ if you wish. I am sure if we work together, ___ will benefit!

Comments

New Child (continued)

Comments for Students

Welcome to School! We are glad to have you here and are looking forward to getting to know you better. ___ will be your partner. He will help you find your way around our school.

Welcome to School! I am very happy to have you as part of our class. You will have fun making new friends. I hope we have a chance to visit soon. Would you be able to eat lunch with me tomorrow? I would love to hear about your old school and some of the things that you like to do.

How lucky we are to have you in our classroom! Thanks for telling us about your old school and some of your hobbies. I hope that you will bring your collection in to show us. You have already taught us many things.

Moving Child

I was sorry to hear that ___ is moving. She will be missed. I am sure that ___ will make a good adjustment at her new school.

Our classroom will not be the same without ___! He was a good student and very kind to others. I am sure that he will make a great transition in his new school. Keep in touch. Don't hesitate to call if I can be of help.

We will all miss ___. She should adjust easily to her new school. I have attached a letter to her new teachers listing concepts we have covered this year. I also identified areas of strength and weakness. Good luck to all of you!

Good luck to ___ at his new school! It would be helpful to ___'s new teacher if you brought our last report card. Be sure to let the new school know that he was receiving special services. This will help make a smoother transition. Please let me know if I can be of further help. Keep in touch!

Comments for Students

How lucky your new teacher will be to have you in her class. I will certainly miss your smile and friendly ways. You will do well in your new school. Please write and let us know how things are going. Good luck!

What sad news for us and what good news for your new teacher! It must be very exciting to be moving into your new house. Don't forget your old friends!

Comments

Moving Child (continued)

Comments for Students

Good luck in your new school. Your classmates and I would love to be your pen pals. Write to us, and we will write to you. Remember to be your very best self and you will go far!

I don't know what we will do without you here to share your good ideas. We will certainly miss you, and we wish you well. You will do a fabulous job at your new school. I am sure you will be their math champ in short order.

End of School Year

Thank you for sharing ___ with me this year. I really enjoyed working with her. I am sure she will have a successful year next year. Enjoy your summer.

It was a pleasure to work with ___. I could always count on him to do his very best. Thank you for your cooperation and support this year.

___ had a great year. I really enjoyed watching her grow academically and socially. She did a good job in ___ and will surely do well next year. It might be a good idea to have her practice over the summer to keep her skills sharp. Enjoy your summer!

How quickly this year has gone by! I hope that ___ has a great summer and enjoys the extra time with his family. Consider enrolling ___ in the summer reading program at the library. He will benefit from the extra reading practice and will like the challenge of working for prizes.

Comments for Students

Congratulations on a great year! You have worked hard to be your very best self, and I know that you are ready for next year. I am so proud of the fine citizen that you are and am looking forward to hearing many good things about you in the future. Good luck to you!

You should be very proud of the fine job that you did this year—I know that I am! I wish you all the best in the future. I am sure that you will do a super job. Have a great summer. Stop in to see me next year!

Enjoy your summer. You have worked hard this year to do your best, and I am very proud of you for that. Keep up the good work, and you will have a great year next year.

Comments

End of School Year (continued)

Comments for Students

It was a pleasure to have you in my class this year. I appreciated the way that you helped others and always tried to do your best. Good luck to you next year.

I will certainly miss your great smile next year. Remember to be your best self!

Good luck next year. Remember to check your work before you turn it in. I hope that you join the summer reading program at the library. It will help you keep your reading skills sharp. Have a great summer!

Unpaid Fees

School Fees

My records show that ___'s school fees have not been paid. It is important that these fees are paid so that your accounts can be cleared. If it would be more convenient for you to pay in installments, please call the office and make these arrangements.

Our records indicate that ___'s school fees have not been paid. Unfortunately, his report card will not be released until they are. You will need to call the school office to make special arrangements if you are unable to pay.

Picture Fees

My records show that ___ has not paid for her school pictures. Please send payment or return the packet of pictures. If you have questions or concerns, please feel free to call. Thanks!

I am trying to close the books on this year's school picture project. Unfortunately, I am unable to do so because ___ has not paid for his pictures. Please send payment or return the pictures. Your cooperation is appreciated.

Lunch Fees

___ owes money for lunches. She will be unable to borrow again until this has been paid. Thank you for your cooperation.

___ has borrowed money for lunches on several occasions and has not repaid the cafeteria. He owes money and will not be able to borrow again until this bill has been paid.

Unpaid Fees (continued)

Lunch Fees

As a convenience to our students and their parents, a fund has been set up to lend money to children who have forgotten lunch or milk money. At this time ___ has borrowed money. She must repay this loan before she can borrow again. It is important that we have the money available to lend to others in need. Thank you for your cooperation.

Field Trips

___ has not returned his permission slip or money for our field trip to (destination). He will not be able to accompany the class unless I have his permission slip. Arrangements can be made to assist with the cost of the trip if necessary. Please let me know whether or not ___ has permission to attend by tomorrow, so that I can make the necessary plans.

Thank you for volunteering to go on our field trip to (destination). You will need to bring a packed lunch and beverage. The cost of the trip for adults is (cost). I have assigned six children to be in your group. I will provide a list and name tags on the day of the trip. We are planning to leave the school promptly at (time) and will return at (time). Let me know if you have questions. It should be a great day!

I am so glad you will be able to accompany our class on our trip to (destination) on (date). Our bus will leave the school at (time) and should return at (time). Much of the day will be spent outdoors, so dress accordingly. You will need a bag lunch and beverage. The cost of the trip is (cost). Thank you for volunteering. I appreciate it!

Our class is planning a field trip to (place) on (date) at (time). We will need parent volunteers to help with supervision. Would you be available to help? You would have a group of six to eight students to look after. We have made this trip several times over the years and the students have always enjoyed it very much. I hope you can be part of this year's experience. Please let me know!

Comments-at-a-Glance

Are you looking for the right word or phrase to convey your thoughts? Read below to find a list of appropriate adjectives and short phrases that you can use in comments to parents or students.

Encouraging Words

Beautiful job!
Don't give up now!
Great discovery!
Great effort!
Great start!
Good attempt!
Good for you!
Good job!
Keep on going!
Keep trying!
Keep up the good work!
I am proud of you!
I believe in you!
I know you can do it!
I appreciate you!
Nice work!
Remarkable!
Right on target!
Sensational improvement!
Stick to it!
Super work!
Way to go!
What a star thinker!
You are special!
You figured it out!
You have improved!
You made a difference!
You made my day!
You really shine!
Your work is awesome!
You're amazing!
You're on the right track!
You've got it!

Well Done

Ambitious
Artistic
Beautiful
Bright
Capable
Cheerful
Clear-thinking
Consistent
Cooperative
Courteous
Creative
Dependable
Eager
Energetic
Enthusiastic
Exceptional
Fabulous
Fair
Fantastic
Friendly
Gifted
Hardworking
Imaginative
Marvelous
Outstanding
A pleasure
Progressing nicely
Superb
Talented
Terrific
Self-Confident
Showing growth
Well-mannered

Needs Improvement

Aggressive
Bossy
Careless
Daydreamer
Dependent
Disobedient
Disorganized
Disruptive
Hasty
Impolite
Impulsive
Inattentive
Inconsistent
Insecure
Irresponsible
Is not applying himself/herself
Lacks concentration
Messy
Needs constant reminding
Needs to listen
Needs to practice
Not working to potential
Talkative
Restless
Rude
Rushes through work
Shy
Temperamental
Thoughtless
Unproductive
Unreliable
Unsocial
Untruthful